The Conveyancers' Yearbook 2005

Russell Hewitson LLB

Solicitor and Principal Lecturer in Law, Northumbria University
Property Law Consultant with Harvey & Marron, Solicitors,
Newcastle-upon-Tyne

Published by **Shaw & Sons Limited**

Shaw's
Since 1750

Published by
Shaw & Sons Limited
Shaway House
21 Bourne Park
Bourne Road
Crayford
Kent DA1 4BZ

© Shaw & Sons Limited 2005

Published June 2005

ISBN 0 7219 1567 1
ISSN 1462-8201

A CIP catalogue record for this book is available from the
British Library

*No part of this publication may be reproduced or
transmitted in any form without the written permission of
the copyright holder*

Printed in Great Britain by
Athenæum Press Ltd., Gateshead, Tyne & Wear

CONTENTS

Contents

Contents

Contents

ALPHABETICAL LIST OF CASES

Alphabetical list of cases

PREFACE

The purpose of this book is to provide conveyancers across all branches of the legal profession and other professionals involved in the property world with a summary of the main changes which have happened over the past year. The book is not intended to be comprehensive and is not a substitute for a textbook, nor for more detailed reading. It merely aims to provide a quick-reference guide to the major developments in conveyancing over that period. As such, it contains a summary of the most important court decisions, ranging over a broad field of conveyancing and landlord and tenant law. The choice of cases is necessarily subjective but it is hoped that those included in the text will be both useful and of interest to the reader.

The remaining sections of the book give a brief resumé of changes in the areas of statute law, other recent developments, a look at what the future holds and a reference section which contains a list of new publications, recently published articles and the addresses of some useful web sites. Websites are notorious for changing their addresses without notice, but the addresses given were correct at the date of publication.

My thanks go to Crispin Williams at Shaws for his patience and help in preparing the book for publication. As always, a special note of thanks is due to my wife Andrea for her support and encouragement during the writing of this book. Finally, the book is dedicated to my daughter, Dominique.

As ever, the responsibility for any errors found in the book remains with the author!

The law is stated as at 1 March 2005 though I have been able, with the publisher's indulgence, to incorporate one or two subsequent changes.

Russell Hewitson
Cleadon Village, Sunderland

THE AUTHOR

Russell Hewitson is a solicitor and Principal Lecturer in Law at the University of Northumbria at Newcastle. He specialises in Conveyancing, Landlord and Tenant Law, and Licensing Law and has lectured extensively on these subjects. He is the author of *Business Tenancies* (Blackstone Press Ltd), *Liquor Licensing and Young Persons* (Northumbria Law Press) and co-author of *Blackstone's Guide to Landlord and Tenant Covenants: Understanding the New Law* and *Conveyancing in Practice* (Northumbria Law Press).

THE LAW REPORTS AND ABBREVIATIONS REFERRED TO IN PART A

All ER .... All England Law Reports

Ch .... Chancery Law Reports

EG .... Estates Gazette

EGCS .... Estates Gazette Case Summary

EGLR .... Estates Gazette Law Reports

EWCA .... England and Wales Court of Appeal

EWHC .... England and Wales High Court

HLR .... Housing Law Reports

L & TR .... Landlord & Tenant Review

P & CR .... Property & Compensation Reports

UKHL .... United Kingdom House of Lords

WLR .... Weekly Law Reports

Part A

RECENT CASES

1 BOUNDARIES

1.1 Joyce v Rigolli

[2004] EWCA Civ 79; [2004] 1 P & CR DG22

The facts:

The case involved a dispute about the boundary between land belonging to the parties. Mr Rigolli claimed that the boundary had been fixed in a transfer between Mrs Joyce and his predecessor in title and in a later informal boundary agreement which had resulted in a small exchange of land between the two plots. Mrs Joyce claimed that Mr Rigolli's fence and garage encroached on her property. The judge found for Mr Rigolli and held that the parties had orally reached a binding agreement with regard to the line of the boundary between their properties. Mrs Joyce appealed and argued that the boundary agreement ought to have been in writing as required by section 2 of the Law of Property (Miscellaneous Provisions) Act 1989 and also that there was no consideration for the boundary agreement.

The decision:

The Court of Appeal found in favour of Mr Rigolli. Section 2 did not apply to trivial dispositions of land consciously made pursuant to an informal boundary agreement of the demarcating kind. Consideration was given by Mr Rigolli's promise to be bound by the agreement. It was impossible to determine the boundary from the plans which were drawn to a small scale.

Comment:

Notwithstanding this decision, it should always be best practice to ensure that these types of agreement comply with section 2 and that notice of the agreement is registered at the Land Registry. Section 2 requires contracts for the sale or other disposition of land to be in writing, to incorporate all the terms that the parties have expressly agreed in one document or, where contracts are to be exchanged, in each document, and to be signed by or on behalf of each party.

The court also considered the position if section 2 did apply to the boundary agreement. The court found that the circumstances for proprietary estoppel existed. There had been an agreement as to the position of the boundary and this had been acted on by the parties. Therefore, a constructive trust had arisen which is not affected by section 2.

Consideration may also be given, in a situation such as this, whether to ask the Land Registry to fix the boundary, which would then prevent a neighbouring owner from acquiring title by adverse possession. One of the situations in which registered boundaries can change is where a neighbour adversely possesses land not in his registered title and for ten years of his adverse possession reasonably believes that he owns it. However, it is not possible to acquire title in this way if the boundary has been fixed.

1.2 Seeckts v Derwent

[2004] EWCA Civ 393; [2004] NPC 51

The facts:

The defendant appealed against the decision that the claimant was the owner of a hedge which had been destroyed by the defendant. The claimant had been awarded damages and an injunction to restrain further trespass by the defendant. The immediate cause of proceedings was the destruction by the defendant of a length of laurel hedge which divided his property, Linden House, from Clock House, which was owned by the claimant. The division of the two properties dated back to a 1968 conveyance. The ownership of the hedge turned on the construction of this conveyance and the plan attached to it. The essential difference between the parties' contentions came down to the choice, in the 1968 conveyance plan, between the dimensions and the 'T' marks as the determinative features. The defendant contended that the judge had not given sufficient weight to the dimensions.

The decision:

The difficulty with the defendant's approach was that it gave no effect to the 'T' marks. It was not possible to disregard the ordinary understanding of the 'T' marks. The natural implication was that they were intended to represent existing boundary features and that those features belonged to the claimant. This implication was consistent with the judge's finding (for which there was evidence) that there was a hedge along the disputed boundary. It was also consistent with the replies to the pre-contract enquiries. The dimensions did not give a sufficiently clear indication to displace the natural implication of the 'T' marks. The likely explanation was that the dimensions were intended to provide a general indication of the boundary but not to detract from the implication of the 'T' marks that the boundary features belonged to the claimant. The judge came to the right conclusion and the appeal on the main issues failed.

Comment:

There was no material dispute in the case as to the significance of 'T' marks in general, and the evidence of the claimant's surveyor that 'the Clock House boundaries are marked with 'T' symbols positioned inwards which, in accordance with normally recognised convention, and without specific evidence to the contrary, would show any feature on the boundary to be in the ownership of Clock House', was repeated in the judgment of Carnwarth LJ at paragraph 15.

2 BREAK CLAUSE

2.1 John Laing Construction Ltd v Amber Pass Ltd

[2004] 2 EGLR 128

The facts:

In 1988 the tenant was granted a lease of an office block in Hemel Hempstead. The lease contained a break clause entitling the tenant to determine the lease at the end of the fifteenth year of the term by serving 6 months' written notice on the landlord, expiring at the end of that year, together with the payment of 12 months' rent and 'upon yielding up of the entirety of the demised premises'. In 2001 the tenant decided that it no longer needed the premises and gradually began to vacate them. When the tenant informed its landlord that it had almost vacated the premises, the landlord expressed concerns about the security of the premises. The tenant therefore arranged security and placed additional free-standing fencing and barriers at the vacant premises. The tenant then sent formal notice under the lease of its intention to determine the lease and subsequently sought a declaration that it had terminated the lease. The landlord argued that the presence of security guards, the use of barriers and the fact that the tenant had not formally returned the keys meant that it had not 'yielded up' the premises for the purpose of the lease. Further, the landlord argued that 'yielding up' meant 'handing back', which required an overt act by the tenant. The absence of authority as to what 'yielding up' meant demonstrated that there should be an obvious event which could not be mistaken for anything else. The tenant argued that 'yielding

4

up' referred to leaving the premises so that the landlord could re-enter them in circumstances where it was clear that the tenant no longer sought a right to the premises, and that the tenant was not required to go through a ceremony of handing back the keys.

The decision:

There was no prescribed form or procedure for 'yielding up'. The court had to look at the facts objectively and determine whether there had been a clear intention by the person whose acts were said to have brought about a termination to effect such termination and whether the landlord could, if he wanted to, occupy the premises without difficulty or objection. The tenant's retention of the keys did not signify any intention on its part to assert any rights in respect of the premises. In the light of security problems at the site, the instruction of security staff and the use of removable concrete barriers did not cause a hindrance to the landlord. The tenant had clearly and obviously demonstrated a wish to terminate the lease. It had served a valid notice and had done as much as was necessary to show the landlord that it asserted no right to the premises and had left it to the landlord to occupy or deal with as it wished.

Comment:

This decision is consistent with a number of earlier cases in which it was held that the retention of keys is not, of itself, an assertion or acceptance of a right to occupy premises.

2.2 Harbour Estates Ltd v HSBC Bank plc

[2004] EWHC 1714; [2004] 3 All ER 1057

The facts:

A lease of business premises on the Isle of Dogs was granted to Stafford Properties Ltd for a term from 24 June 1993 to 24 December 2013. The lease contained a break clause entitling the tenant to terminate the lease on 23 June 1999, 23 June 2004 or 23 June 2009 on giving not less than six months' notice to the landlord. The break clause was expressed to be personal to Stafford. Stafford subsequently assigned the lease to its parent company, HSBC. HSBC sent the landlord a notice purporting to terminate the lease in accordance with the break clause on 23 June 2004. The landlord claimed that the notice was invalid, arguing that it did not 'touch and concern the land' but was personal to Stafford and was therefore incapable of assignment, neither had the benefit of the break clause been expressly assigned to HSBC. HSBC argued that the benefit of the break right had passed automatically on the assignment of the lease by virtue of section 63 of the Law of Property Act 1925, which provides that a conveyance passes 'all the estate, right, title, interest, claim, and demand which the conveying parties respectively have, in, to or on' the property conveyed.

The decision:

The benefit of the break clause passed automatically to HSBC with the assignment of the lease. The break clause was a right 'in, to, or on the property conveyed' and thus not wholly a personal right. Section 63 did not expressly refer to any test of annexation or 'touching and concerning'. Further, the lease clearly contemplated other classes of tenant who might acquire the benefit of the clause. Nor was there anything in the clause to suggest that, after an assignment of the lease, the assignor should be able to regulate whether the benefit passed on subsequent assignments or that the landlord should have the power to prevent its passing automatically to a subsequent assignee. It followed that HSBC had the benefit of the break clause and had validly exercised it.

Comment:

Section 63 is rarely encountered in practice. It is not effective to carry an entirely separate hereditament and it can, in any event, be excluded by an express contrary wording in the deed. The judge was able to find that the break clause in this case was not wholly personal and that it was open to him to regard it as 'touching and concerning'. However, it is not entirely clear from the case whether the judge considered that section 63 has such a limited application, despite the fact that its wording appears not to require it. In practice it would be advisable for the assignment of the lease to include a separate express assignment of the benefit of the break right.

3 BUSINESS TENANCIES

3.1 Pennycook v Shaws (EAL) Ltd

[2004] EWCA Civ 100; [2004] 2 All ER 665

The facts:

The tenancy was subject to Part II of the Landlord and Tenant Act 1954 and the landlord served a section 25 notice to terminate the tenancy. The tenant erroneously served a positive counter-notice. Before the period for serving the counter-notice expired, the tenant served a negative counter-notice and applied for a new tenancy in the county court. The application was struck out on the grounds that the service of the counter-notice did not invalidate the positive counter-notice and that section 29 prevented the court from considering the application for a new tenancy without a valid negative counter-notice. The tenant obtained permission to appeal on human rights grounds and the court decided that it was entitled to give a second counter-notice. On appeal, the landlord argued that the High Court was bound to follow the interpretation of section 25 and section 29(2) in *Re 14 Grafton Street, London W1* ([1971] Ch 935). The tenant countered that that interpretation breached the Human Rights Act 1998 (Schedule 1, Part II, Article 1 and Schedule 1, Part I, Article 6(1)).

The decision:

The appeal was allowed. Section 3 of the 1998 Act did not require the court to depart from the decision in *14 Grafton Street* when interpreting section 25 and section 29(2) of the 1954 Act. That interpretation allowed a landlord to rely on a positive counter-notice on the basis that the counter-notice provided certainty. Even though that interpretation could cause hardship in some cases, there was no breach of Schedule 1, Part II, Article 1. Article 6(1) did not apply, as the bar to relying on the second negative counter-notice was substantive and there was no reason why an application should be heard on the basis of the 1998 Act when it fell to be dismissed under section 25 and section 29(2) of the 1954 Act.

Comment:

The result is that notices are irrevocable. The basis of the Court of Appeal's decision leaves the matter far more open to question. However, it is unlikely that a matter such as this will ever reach the House of Lords, as counter-notices have been abolished with effect from 1 June 2004. The more general issue relating to other notices under the 1954 Act will still be of importance.

3.2 Brighton and Hove City Council v Collinson

[2004] EWCA Civ 678; [2004] 2 EGLR 65

The facts:

The council had entered into negotiations with two brothers for their company to lease premises in a leisure centre. The parties agreed to exclude the security of tenure provisions in the 1954 Act. An application for a contracting out order was allowed in the company's name, with the brothers as sureties, but the lease was ultimately entered into by the brothers. The county court decided that the lease had not been excluded from Part II of the Landlord and Tenant Act 1954. The council appealed.

The decision:

The appeal was allowed. Section 38(4)(a) of the 1954 Act was not to be given an overly complex interpretation and there was no reason why an application to exclude security of tenure could not include all parties to the lease negotiations. The brothers had been parties to the application and understood that they were giving up security of tenure protection, and there was substantial similarity between the draft and final leases with the change in tenant being made for tax purposes.

Comment:

This case makes it clear that relatively significant amendments can still be made to the lease without affecting the validity of a contracting out order. However, this is only relevant to existing leases. Under the new contracting out rules it is necessary, before exchange of agreements, to serve a notice containing the 'health warning' and for the tenant to make either a declaration or Statutory Declaration. If there are very significant changes from the form of lease set out in the agreement, the appropriate course is to have a variation of the original agreement, which would have to be preceded by the notices and declarations under the new rules.

3.3 Parsons v George

[2004] EWCA Civ 912; [2004] 3 All ER 633

The facts:

A business tenant appealed against the refusal of his application to amend out of time his claim for a new tenancy under the Landlord and Tenant Act 1954. The landlord had died and the tenant had erroneously served his claim form on the late landlord's executors rather than the person to whom they had transferred the freehold. The tenant applied to substitute the transferee's name as defendant to the claim. The judge held that he had no power under the Civil Procedure Rules 1998, rule 19, to allow the amendment, as the 1954 Act was not an enactment that satisfied the requirements of rule 19.5(1)(c). On appeal, the tenant contended that the judge had erred in his interpretation of rule 19.

The decision:

The appeal was allowed and the amendment allowed. The judge's interpretation of rule 19.5 effected a very significant reduction in the jurisdiction, to allow the addition or substitution of parties after the expiry of a relevant limitation period when compared with the previous court procedure rules. That was not the intention behind the amendment introduced by rule 19.5(1)(c), which had to be given a broad interpretation to include any statute that allowed or did not prohibit a change of parties after the relevant limitation period. The 1954 Act fell into the latter category, therefore the application came within rule 19.5. Rule 19.3(a) also had to be approached broadly, to include situations where a genuine mistake had been made as to the identity of a party. The tenant had issued proceedings against the executors in the mistaken belief that they were the competent landlords. Both the executors and the transferee had had the same solicitors throughout and there was no question of there being any prejudice to either in making the amendment. This was a clear case in which discretion should be exercised in favour of granting the application to amend.

Comment:

This is a welcome decision as it clarifies the issue as to whether the CPR retained the Rules of the Supreme Court's jurisdiction to permit amendments after the expiry of a limitation period, where a statute is silent, as to whether such amendments are permitted. This is a matter of some importance given that over 50 statutes fall into this category. It also clarifies the nature of CPR rule 19.

3.4 Davy's of London (Wine Merchants) Ltd v City of London Corporation

[2004] EWHC 2224; [2004] 49 EG 136

The facts:

The tenant held the lease of a wine bar for a term of 25 years expiring in March 2002. The landlord did not oppose the tenant's request for a new tenancy. At the hearing of the tenant's application, the county court judge had concluded that:

a) the building containing the premises required extensive refurbishment, and this could not take place while the tenant was in occupation;

b) at the date of the hearing, the landlord did not intend to carry out the works itself, but was to sell the building to a developer that intended to redevelop it;

c) the assembly of a site for redevelopment would be in excess of three years (the island site scheme);

d) no planning permission had been submitted for the redevelopment; and

e) the proposed redevelopment would not be viable.

The judge ordered that a new 14-year tenancy be granted, with a rolling redevelopment break clause exercisable on 11 months' notice after the first five years of the term. Both parties appealed. Prior to the hearing of the appeal, the landlord sold the building to a developer, which intended to redevelop the building as a stand-alone development. It was ordered that the developer be joined in to the proceedings and that the new evidence be adduced.

The decision:

The county court judge had applied the correct legal test in considering whether a redevelopment break clause should be inserted in the new tenancy. The test involved two propositions, namely that, so far as reasonable, a new tenancy should not prevent a landlord from developing, and a reasonable degree of security of tenure should be provided to the tenant. The decision of the county court judge may have been at the borders of his discretion, in selecting five years before the break clause was exercisable, but he did not exceed it. The question as to whether fresh evidence could be admitted in an appeal after the trial is a discretionary matter for the court. Since the new evidence was challenged on behalf of the tenant, and the developer gave disclosure of a number of documents, the appeal was an appeal by way of a rehearing. The relevant date for the purpose of determining the terms of the tenancy was the date of the appeal. On the facts, the developer's intention was to assemble the island site scheme, and not to develop the subject building on its own. However, in the light of the new evidence, the break clause should be exercisable on 11 months' notice and should not be served prior to 1 July 2007.

Comment:

The decision shows that post-trial evidence can be admitted where the court cannot conscientiously deal with an appeal without reference to it.

4 COMMON LAND

4.1 R (on the application of Whitmey) v Commons Commissioners

[2004] EWCA Civ 951; [2004] 3 WLR 1343

The facts:

The appellant appealed against a refusal to grant permission to bring proceedings for judicial review, in respect of a decision of the commons commissioners that they had no jurisdiction to consider disputed applications for the registration of land as a town or village green under the Commons Registration Act 1965. The appellant was a director and trustee of a charity that owned the disputed land. An application was made pursuant to register it as a village green on the basis of 20 years use for lawful sports and pastimes. A notice of objection was subsequently sent to the registration authority. Neither the Act nor the Commons Registration (New Land) Regulations 1969 prescribed a procedure for resolving such disputed applications. It was the practice of registration authorities to have the dispute decided by a committee of elected members, or to arrange for a public inquiry to be held by an independent expert whose role would be to provide a report and recommendation to the registration authority. The appellant sought to refer the disputed application to register the village green to the commons commissioners.

The decision:

The process of deciding disputed applications adopted by the registration authorities did not infringe Article 6 of the European Convention on Human Rights. Any decision to register could clearly be reviewed by the courts under the Act. The decision whether to register a piece of land as a green after a public inquiry was similar to a planning decision. The controls on the decisions of planning inspectors effected by the availability of subsequent judicial review had been held to comply fully with the requirements of Article 6. As the powers envisaged by the Act were wider than would be the case on judicial review, it was clear that the procedure for the registration of greens complied with Article 6. Moreover, as the Act and the Regulations did not identify procedures for resolving disputes of the instant nature, there was nothing to prevent a landowner, who objected to his land being registered, bringing proceedings in court to obtain a declaration prior to registration.

Comment:

The Commons Commissioners have no jurisdiction to hear a dispute as to whether or not a village green should be registered under section 13 of the Commons Registration Act 1965.

5 CONSENT TO ASSIGN

5.1 NCR Ltd v Riverland Portfolio No 1 Ltd (No 1)

[2004] EWHC 921; [2005] 1 P & CR 3

The facts:

The claimant was the tenant of office premises let by the defendant. Under the lease, the annual rent of £338,000 was to be reviewed every five years on an upwards-only basis. The annual rent since 1990 had been £710,000. By clause 3.11 of the lease, the claimant covenanted '... not to underlet the whole of the demised premises or permit any underlease of the whole of the demised premises to be derived directly or indirectly ... out of this lease unless (i) the underlease is granted at the best rent obtainable in the open market without the grantor taking any premium or other capital consideration or, if greater, the rent then payable thereunder...'. The claimant proposed to underlease the premises and the proposed subtenant was willing, in compliance with clause 3.11, to pay an annual rent of £710,000 but, as the rent was in excess of the market rent, it required the claimant to pay it a reverse premium of £3,000,000. The defendant refused to consent to the underlease, arguing that taking into account the premium, the proposed rent was less than the market rent. It submitted that the premium was disguised rent which, when split between the residue of the term and the reduced rent, meant that the true annual rent payable under the proposed underlease would be approximately £210,000, which was half the open market rent and one-third of the rent payable under the lease. The claimant sought a declaration that the proposed underlease was authorised by the lease.

The decision:

The reverse premium did not infringe the terms of the head lease. The court distinguished the decision in *Allied Dunbar Assurance plc v Homebase Ltd* ([2002] EWCA Civ 666), which turned on the construction of particular documents before the court at the time, from which it was dangerous, particularly in landlord and tenant matters, to derive general principles of law. A significant difference was that, in *Allied Dunbar*, the figures in the underlease were based on an entirely fictional calculation. In the present case there was no justification for treating the capital payment as being anything other than a premium. Without any challenge to the documentation, it was not permissible for the court to rewrite an underlease and change a premium into a figure and incorporate it as rent. On the facts, the obligations contained in the underlease were substantially in excess of what would be the open market value of a new lease. A genuine reverse premium could not be a breach of clause 3.11 and the claimant was entitled to a declaration.

Comment:

The court managed to split the premium from the rent and, unlike in *Allied Dunbar*, was not prepared to construe the bargain between the parties as being one for a reduced rent. The reverse premium could not be treated in the same way as a collateral deed and was a separate payment which did not affect the rent which the subtenant would pay. It is clear that each case will turn on its own facts and that a premium must be genuine and not a sham.

5.2 Design Progression Ltd v Thurloe Properties Ltd

[2004] EWHC 324; [2004] 2 P & CR 31

The facts:

On 21 January 2002 the tenant applied for a licence to assign its lease. Within two months of making the application, it had provided the landlord with trading and management accounts and references in respect of the proposed assignee, who was an experienced businesswoman. Three months after the receipt of the application, the landlord had failed to communicate any decision. The tenant claimed damages under section 1(3) of the Landlord and Tenant Act 1988 for the landlord's failure to respond within a reasonable time to its application for consent to assign a lease.

The decision:

The landlord was in breach of its obligation to give a decision on the application within a reasonable time. Two months after the date of the application, it had been in possession of all the information necessary to enable it to make a decision as to whether or not to give licence to assign, but had failed to do so. The landlord was in breach of its obligation at that stage, and was clearly in breach after a further month had elapsed. Had the assignment taken place two months after the application, the tenant would have received a premium of £75,000 and would have been relieved of any further obligation to pay rent, and its claims for the loss of the premium and profits, and in respect of the rental, were properly claimable. The tenant also had a right to claim exemplary damages against a landlord for breach of its statutory duty under section 1(3) of the Act. The landlord had operated in a cynical way designed to frustrate the tenant, and had sought to make a profit by abusing the procedures under the 1988 Act in order to see off the assignee with a view to recovering the premises and extracting a higher rent on the open market. The sum of £25,000 would be awarded by way of exemplary damages.

Comment:

This is yet another case which makes it clear that a landlord must comply with the 1988 Act or risk having to pay damages and possibly exemplary damages.

5.3 Norwich Union Linked Life Assurance Ltd v Mercantile Credit Co Ltd

[2003] EWHC 3064; [2004] 4 EG 109 (CS)

The facts:

The claimant had attempted to sublet premises for which consent was required from both the defendant and the head lessee. The claimant alleged that it had made a request for consent by a letter, addressed to the defendant's solicitors and faxed to the defendant's agents, and that the defendant had unreasonably delayed or withheld its consent so that the sublet was aborted. The claimant claimed damages for the loss suffered under section 1(3) of the Landlord and Tenant Act 1988 or for breach of an alleged covenant in the lease. The underlease contained a covenant not to sublet without the previous consent of the landlord that would not unreasonably be withheld. The covenant was subject to a proviso that the landlord should be satisfied as to the level of rent proposed in the underlease. In its defence, the defendant argued that to give efficacy to that provision, a request for consent to a subletting should stipulate the proposed rent. It also argued that the letter which the claimant sent did not amount to a proper request for consent under the 1988 Act, or under the Landlord and Tenant Act 1927.

The decision:

The court held that the landlord's contention that any request for consent to underlet had to state the proposed rent had no reasonable prospect of success, and should be struck out from the defence. It was a matter for the landlord whether it was concerned with the level of rent and whether it exercised the right granted by the proviso. It was therefore for the landlord in those circumstances to request details of the rent. The landlord also contended that the tenant had failed to comply with section 5(2) of the Landlord and

Tenant Act 1988, by failing to serve its application for consent either by a means provided for in the lease or in accordance with section 23 of the Landlord and Tenant Act 1927. The court held that this aspect was not bound to fail and so should not be struck out.

Comment:

Earlier cases suggest that if a landlord wants further information, he must make his request clearly and promptly. Also, the 1988 Act requires service of the application, in the above sense, on 'the person who may consent' and this must not be overlooked by a tenant seeking to place reliance upon the statutory duties imposed by the Act.

5.4   First Penthouse Ltd v Channel Hotels & Properties (UK) Ltd

[2004] EWCA Civ 1072; [2004] L & TR 27

The facts:

The freeholder granted a development lease of the roof space to a developer who covenanted to carry out, and complete, a development project as expeditiously as possible. The developer subsequently charged the lease to the mortgagee. The freeholder subsequently granted an overriding lease to the landlord. At a time when neither the developer nor the mortgagee had the means to complete the development project, the developer sought consent to assign the lease to the tenant who did have means. The landlord refused consent, and the developer proceeded with the assignment. The mortgagee sought a declaration that the landlord's consent had been unreasonably withheld. The landlord brought proceedings seeking to establish its entitlement to forfeit the lease. As a preliminary matter, the judge held that the breach of the covenant to develop expeditiously was a once and for all breach, and that the landlord had waived its entitlement to forfeit on that basis by its conduct, and in particular by its demand for and acceptance of rent. The landlord appealed.

The decision:

It was held that a covenant to do something by a particular date was a covenant that could only be broken once. This also applied to a covenant to do something within a reasonable time. In this case, it was possible to point to a time by which the works, if carried out and completed as expeditiously as possible, should have been completed. The covenant, therefore, recognised a once and for all breach. The judge had also been correct in finding that consent to assign had been unreasonably withheld.

Comment:

The doctrine of waiver causes few problems in practice for a landlord faced with a breach of covenant by his tenant that amounts to a continuing breach, for example a breach of a covenant to repair. However, where a once and for all breach occurs, if the landlord is to retain a right of forfeiture it is essential that he does nothing that may be construed as a recognition of the continuing existence of the lease.

5.5   Old English Inns plc v Brightside Ltd

The Times, June 30, 2004

The facts:

The claimants were tenants of the Hinds Head public house and restaurant in Bray and sought declarations that their landlord, the defendant, had unreasonably delayed its consent to the assignment of the premises, and that they were entitled to assign. The proposed assignee was a company owned by the well-known chef, Heston Blumenthal, of the Fat Duck (also in Bray), and who had three Michelin stars. The main issue for determination was whether or not the proposed assignee was financially sound, as this was expressly required by the lease. Another issue arose as to whether the requirement was a condition precedent.

The decision:

The proposed assignee was financially sound. It was artificial in the case of a small one-man, or two-person, private company to look solely at the balance sheet and profit and loss account crude figures in deciding whether or not it was financially sound. It was wholly artificial and did not accord with commercial reality to hold that the financial soundness of such a company turned on what policy was adopted on the part of the directors in relation to their drawings, when that historic policy could immediately be altered if necessary. It was wholly legitimate to take into account that the proposed assignee's debts were guaranteed by guarantors who were willing and able to meet their guarantee and who, by means of this guarantee, would ensure that the company had sufficient working capital from the bank. The proposed assignee had sufficient funding to meet its ongoing financial requirements for the foreseeable future. Since the Landlord and Tenant (Covenants) Act 1995, one should start by looking to see whether a lease specified circumstances in which the landlord could withhold his consent and, if it did so, apply section 19(1)(a) of the Landlord and Tenant Act 1927 straightforwardly, without entering into an analysis of the wording to see whether it created a condition precedent which operated anteriorly to the coming into operation of the covenant against assignment without consent. In any event, the requirement was not a condition precedent.

Comment:

The judge rejected the landlord's claim that the assignment would reduce the value of its reversion. He took the view that the landlord had no intention at all of selling the reversion, and that it would much prefer to buy the lease itself. He also ruled that the landlord's objection had no basis in fact or law, and that the landlord had failed to cite this as a reason for refusing to consent to the assignment at the time when it should have done so, and that it was too late to raise this now.

6   CONTRACTS

6.1   Nweze v Nwoko

[2004] EWCA Civ 379: [2004] 2 P & CR 33

The facts:

In December 2000, the respondent agreed to sell a house to the appellant. The price orally agreed was £135,000. On completion, part of the purchase price was left outstanding and, in 2002, a meeting was held to resolve the dispute between the parties as to payment for the property. A further oral agreement was reached for the property to be sold at the best price obtainable and for the proceeds to be paid to the respondent to discharge the outstanding balance. The appellant declined to proceed with the sale and the respondent issued proceedings to enforce the original sale agreement at the orally agreed price of £135,000 and, in the alternative, to enforce the compromise agreement. The court held that the original agreement could not be enforced by virtue of section 2 of the Law of Property (Miscellaneous Provisions) Act 1989, but that the oral compromise agreement was enforceable as it was not caught by section 2. The appellant now appealed against this decision.

The decision:

The appeal was dismissed. Section 2 was concerned with agreements under which there was a seller on one side and a buyer on the other. In this case, the agreement was not a contract for the sale of the property, nor a contract for the disposition of any interest in the property between the parties. Nor was it a contract for the sale of the property or the disposition of any interest in the property to any third party. It was simply a contract under which the appellant was obliged to enter into such a contract if a buyer was found. Under the compromise agreement, the respondent did not gain a legal or equitable interest in the property. Without the marketing of the property there could be no sale or disposition, and it would be a misuse of language to say that the compromise was a contract for the sale or disposition of an interest in land.

Comment:

Section 2 applies to contracts to carry out future transactions and does not apply to the documents completing the transaction, for example a transfer. It should not be assumed that failure to comply with section 2 will always be fatal, and a check should be made as to the nature of the arrangements that have been entered into to clarify whether they fall within the scope of section 2.

6.2 BP Oil UK Ltd v Lloyds TSB Bank plc

[2004] EWCA Civ 1710; [2005] 10 EG 156

The facts:

The defendant assigned a 25-year lease of office premises to the three claimant companies. The contract included a put option, stated to be 'personal and non-assignable', under which the claimants, as the 'Purchaser', could require the defendant to take back the property by way of assignment in either September 2004 or September 2010. In March 2003, the claimants sent a notice to the defendant purporting to exercise the option as of September 2004. At that time, only two of the three claimant companies were tenants under the lease. The defendant maintained that, in such circumstances, the claimants were not entitled to exercise the option. It also claimed that it was too late to re-assign the property to all three claimants, in order to overcome the problem, because the earlier assignment had rendered the option incapable of being exercised, regardless of subsequent events. The claimants brought proceedings to determine whether the option had been validly exercised by the March notice and, if not, whether the option could be validly exercised if the lease were re-assigned to all three companies. The judge determined the first issue in favour of the defendant and the second issue in favour of the claimants. Both parties appealed.

The decision:

The appeals were dismissed. The judge had been correct in his interpretation of the agreement. The word 'personal' in the put option meant something additional to 'not capable of assignment'. Given the background to the put option, and the fact that it was in a separate agreement, that interpretation was consistent with the commercial aims of the parties. Accordingly, all three claimants, being 'the Purchaser' as defined by the option agreement, had to exercise the option without any direction from a third party. Further, at the time of giving notice of exercise, the claimants, on the natural interpretation of the option agreement, had to be the registered proprietors of the lease. Otherwise, they would be able to exercise the put option at the request of an assignee, and such exercise would not be for their own benefit. However, it would be stretching the option agreement too far to say that the 'Purchaser' had to have retained exactly the same interest in the lease throughout the period of the agreement. The put option did not permanently cease to be exercisable when the lease ceased to be vested in the claimants. It became exercisable again when the lease was revested in the claimant companies.

Comment:

This a common sense decision. If a provision is personal it should be available to the relevant person, whether as the original tenant or on re-assignment. If a right is to lapse on assignment, the lease should say so.

6.3 Kinane v Mackie-Conteh

[2005] EWCA Civ 45; [2005] 6 EG 140 (CS)

The facts:

The respondent agreed to make a loan of £50,000 to a company, of which the appellant was managing director, in order to enable it to take advantage of a business opportunity. As security for the loan, the appellant and his wife signed a letter agreeing that the respondent could place a charge over their home for the full amount. The business transaction fell through, and the loan was not repaid. The respondent brought proceedings seeking specific performance of the security agreement. He argued, first, that although the agreement did not comply with the formality requirements of section 2(1) of the Law of Property (Miscellaneous Provisions) Act 1989, it created a constructive trust and therefore fell within the exception set out in section 2(5), and, secondly, that the agreement complied with section 53(1)(c) of the Law of Property Act 1925, being a disposal in writing of an 'equitable interest or trust subsisting at the time of the disposition'. The appellant argued that the agreement was unenforceable under either provision. The judge held that the security agreement was enforceable under section 53(1)(c), but not under section 2 of the 1989 Act. The appellant appealed and the respondent cross-appealed.

The decision:

Section 53(1)(c) could not apply because it was well established that it only applied to subsisting equitable interests. The security agreement was clearly an agreement to create a charge and it was not, therefore, an immediate charge. A constructive trust arose and the respondent could rely on section 2(5) of the 1989 Act. The respondent had acted, to his detriment, in reliance on a belief permitted or encouraged by the appellant that he was to obtain an interest in land in circumstances where it was unconscionable for the appellant not to confer that interest.

Comment:

This is an interesting decision. The respondent had made it clear that he required security for his loan, and the appellant had responded by providing the security agreement and by persuading the respondent that once he had the agreement, he should make the loan. The agreement demonstrated an intention to create a security interest, and the respondent had acted to his detriment by making the loan. The appellant had, by his conduct, encouraged the respondent to believe that the security agreement was valid and binding, and he had to stand by that conduct even if he had misunderstood the effect of section 2(1) of the 1989 Act.

6.4 R (on the application of Khatun) v Newham London Borough Council

[2004] EWCA Civ 55; [2004] 3 WLR 417

The facts:

The respondent had applied to the local authority for accommodation as a homeless person. The local authority made an offer of private sector leased accommodation under the Housing Act 1996 and, in accordance with its policy, required the respondent to accept or decline the accommodation without seeing it. The respondent claimed to have the right to see it first. In judicial review proceedings, the judge held that homeless persons did have such a right and that the local authority's policy was unlawful. The issue arose whether the Unfair Terms in Consumer Contracts Regulations 1999 and the Unfair Contract Terms Directive 93/13/

EEC applied to the terms on which accommodation was let by the local authority and the judge decided as a preliminary issue that they did. The local authority now appealed against this decision.

The decision:

The Unfair Terms in Consumer Contracts Regulations and the Unfair Contract Terms Directive do apply to contracts relating to land and they also apply to public authorities. The Court of Appeal also held that the council is a 'seller or supplier' and the tenant is a 'consumer' within the meaning of the Regulations and the Directive.

Comment:

This decision may potentially have a far-reaching impact in that it opens up for scrutiny the way in which local authority policies are adopted and put into effect. However, the decision in the case was that the local authority's housing policy was neither unlawful nor unreasonable, and was a fair and efficient administration of the scheme under the relevant area of legislation. In the circumstances, the policy was lawful and any challenge to this aspect of the policy was rejected.

6.5 Dandara Holdings Ltd v Co-operative Retail Services Ltd

[2004] EWHC 1476; [2004] 2 EGLR 163

The facts:

The Co-op agreed to sell its headquarters in Rochdale to Dandara. The parties agreed an exclusivity agreement whereby the Co-op would only deal with Dandara for a six-week period. However, during this time, Airtours viewed the property and then made an offer to buy it for a higher price. When the Co-op and Dandara did not exchange contracts within the six weeks, the property was sold to Airtours for the higher price. Dandara claimed damages for loss of the chance of entering into a sale contract at the price originally agreed and therefore loss of the chance of acquiring the property at such a price that it would have been able to make a profit.

The decision:

The delivery of a sales brochure to agents for Airtours during the currency of the exclusivity agreement amounted to a breach of that agreement. The Co-op's agents had mentioned the existence of the agreement to the agents acting for Airtours. However, referring to its existence was not an announcement or publication of the terms of the agreement, nor a comment or statement relating to these terms. Accordingly, there had not been a breach of the agreement by mentioning its existence. The breach occasioned by supply of the sales brochure had no consequence at all, as it had not caused Dandara to lose a substantial chance of becoming the purchaser of the property. Dandara was entitled to recover £22,502.77 in respect of expenses it had incurred for surveys and searches.

Comment:

The decision in this case turned on the facts of the case, but it does illustrate how the courts will approach an alleged breach of an exclusivity agreement, and the difficulties of proving that a breach has caused the buyer to lose a real or substantial chance of purchasing the property.

6.6   Sharif v Sadiq

[2004] EWHC 1913; (2004) 148 SJLB 665

The facts:

The claimant claimed specific performance of a contract for the sale of a property to him by the second defendant for £85,000. The first defendant was the freehold owner of a property which the claimant wished to purchase. The second defendant was the agent of the first defendant and entered into two agreements with the claimant. The first was an oral agreement with the claimant paying a deposit of £8,000 and agreeing that there would be exchange within three months. The second agreement was in writing to the effect that the property would be sold for £85,000 and a completion date was given. The second defendant failed to complete the sale and so the claimant sought specific performance. The second defendant submitted that the agreement was not valid, as the agreement was a contract for the sale of land or for the disposition of an interest in land which did not comply with section 2 of the Law of Property (Miscellaneous Provisions) Act 1989 by not being in writing. The claimant submitted that the contract was not a contract for the sale of land but an agreement to exchange contracts for the sale of land and, therefore, did not need to comply with the provisions of section 2 of the 1989 Act.

The decision:

An agreement to exchange contracts for the sale of land or the disposition of an interest in land could only be made in a form that complied with section 2 of the 1989 Act, as an agreement to exchange contracts gave rise to an equitable interest in land. That had been the position under section 40 of the Law of Property Act 1925 and the changes brought about by the 1989 Act related to substance rather than scope. The changes related to non-compliance, not to the categories of contract for which compliance was required. The instant agreement satisfied the aspect of section 2 requiring the contract to be in writing. However, an enforceable contract only arose if contracts were duly exchanged. The exchange of documents between parties had to constitute more than offer and acceptance but needed to record the express terms of the agreement already made, and it was clear from the evidence that exchange of contracts had not been effected in accordance with section 2 and therefore no contract enforceable by specific performance arose.

Comment:

The buyer's argument that the initial agreement was enforceable, even though it did not comply with section 2 because it did not effect a sale and was simply an agreement to exchange contracts to sell an interest in land, was not successful (compare this with *Nweze v Nwoko* ([2004] EWCA Civ 379; [2004] 2 P & CR 33)). The court considered the facts carefully and went on to rule that the parties may have signed the contracts but that they had not actually exchanged them, because it was not satisfied that either party thought, or intended, or could objectively be understood to have intended, that the seller's agent had agreed to hold the seller's part of the agreement for the buyer. It is also interesting to note that the judge stated that he would have refused an order for specific performance if he had decided that there was a valid contract for the sale of the property, and that he would have left the buyer to his remedy in damages because the buyer had delayed commencing proceedings until just before his action would have been statute-barred.

7   CO-OWNERSHIP

7.1   Bathurst v Scarborow

[2004] EWCA Civ 411; [2005] 1 P & CR 4

The facts:

The appellant appealed against a decision that he had not become beneficial owner of the whole of a partnership property on dissolution of the partnership. The appellant and the respondent had been in partnership in the business of selling darts equipment. There was no written partnership agreement and profits were divided equally. The parties had bought a property using partnership funds as an investment and for storing partnership stock. The transfer stated that they held the property on trust for themselves as joint tenants. After the respondent's death a dispute

29

arose as to whether the right of survivorship applied to the beneficial interests in the property. It was the appellant's case that the property had ultimately been purchased outside the partnership for tax reasons, and that they had specifically agreed to a right of survivorship in respect of the business as a whole and the property in particular. The judge concluded that there was no express agreement between the appellant and the respondent that they would purchase the property outside the partnership and that, consequently, there was no right of survivorship.

The decision:

The appeal was allowed. The judge had erred in viewing the issue solely in terms of whether the property was an asset of the partnership and had not considered whether the appellant and the respondent had agreed to vary the normal rule that property bought with partnership money was deemed to have been bought for the partnership. The appellant bore the burden of proving that a decision had been made to take the property outside the partnership. There was no support for such an argument and all the circumstantial evidence pointed to the property being bought for the partnership. There was no inconsistency between a beneficial joint tenancy and partnership property; the only inconsistency was between the rule of survivorship and the presumption that partnership property was held in common. However, the presumption that partnership property was held in common could be overturned by evidence of an agreement to the contrary. There was clear evidence that the appellant and the respondent had agreed to take the property as beneficial joint tenants in full knowledge of what that would mean.

Comment:

The general rule is that property bought with partnership money belongs to the partnership, and the burden is on the partner who claims otherwise to prove it. There is a presumption that partnership property is held on a tenancy in common, however, if the partners agree, otherwise it will be held on a joint tenancy and the right of survivorship will apply.

7.2 Oxley v Hiscock

[2004] EWCA Civ 546; [2004] 3 All ER 703

The facts:

The parties had had a relationship from the mid-1980s until 2001 but had never married. In 1986, Oxley bought her council house at a discount under the 'right to buy' provisions of the Housing Act 1985. Hiscock provided the whole purchase price of £25,200, which was secured by way of a charge as the property was conveyed into Oxley's sole name. In 1991, the house was sold and the property which was the subject of the current proceedings was purchased in Hiscock's sole name for £127,000 of which £30,000 was provided by way of a loan in Hiscock's name secured by mortgage, £36,300 was contributed by Oxley from the proceeds of sale of the council house and £60,700 was contributed by Hiscock, which included the £25,200 due to him from the previous property. In 2001, the parties separated and the property was sold for £232,000. From the proceeds, Hiscock gave Oxley the equivalent of her original investment in the property, in the region of £36,300, but kept the remainder. Oxley argued that she was entitled to a half share as the intention had always been that the property would be jointly beneficially owned. The judge found for Oxley, holding that such an intention could be inferred from the parties' conduct. On appeal, Hiscock argued that the judge had taken the wrong approach and that Oxley's share should be by way of resulting trust calculated solely on her actual financial contribution.

The decision:

The judge had taken the wrong approach and a fair division of the proceeds was 60% to Hiscock and 40% to Oxley. The authorities in this area of law were to some extent unclear, and the judge had based her decision on a somewhat outdated and 'artificial' approach, in which the conduct of the parties throughout the relationship was used to piece together an inferred intention at the time the property was purchased. Where there was some evidence that the parties had intended some form of shared ownership but had not discussed in what proportion those shares should be, they were each 'entitled to that share which the court considers fair, having regard to the whole course of dealing between them in relation to the property'. The judge had wrongly dwelt on conduct going towards intention instead of stepping back and looking at it from the point of view of overall fairness. Although the parties' cohabitation had involved a 'classic pooling of resources', Hiscock's greater financial contribution had to be taken into account and an equal split would therefore not be fair.

Comment:

When acting on the purchase of a property to be used for joint occupation, a conveyancer must point out the difficulties and advise the parties to make a joint declaration as to the beneficial interests in the property.

8 EASEMENTS

8.1 Bakewell Management Ltd v Brandwood

[2004] UKHL 14; [2004] 2 AC 519

The facts:

The owner of a house which bordered a 144-acre common appealed against the decision that he was not entitled to vehicular access across the common. He had no direct access to his house from a public road and successive owners of the property had used a track across the common for over 20 years. The owner of the common had not given permission authorising this use of the track. Section 193(4) of the Law of Property Act 1925 makes it an offence to drive without lawful authority over a common to which the section applied. The house owner argued that he had acquired a right of way across the common either under section 2 of the Prescription Act 1832 or under the doctrine of the lost modern grant. The Court of Appeal, following the decision in *Hanning v Top Deck Travel Group Ltd* ((1994) 68 P & CR 14), held that he could not have acquired an easement by conduct which, at the time the conduct took place, was prohibited by statute.

The decision:

The appeal was allowed. The decision in *Hanning* was wrong and ought not to be followed. A prescriptive right, or a right under lost modern grant, could be obtained by long use that was illegal in the sense of being tortious. Hanning could only be justified on the basis that conduct which was illegal in a criminal sense was, for public policy purposes, different in kind from conduct illegal in a tortious sense. The use of land made criminal by section 193(4) had much more in common with use of land that was illegal because it was tortious, than with use of land that was illegal because it was criminal. If an easement over land could be lawfully granted by the landowner, the easement could be acquired either by prescription under section 2 of the Prescription Act 1832 or by the fiction of lost modern grant, whether the use relied on was illegal in the criminal sense or illegal merely in the tortious sense.

Comment:

In *Hanning* the Court of Appeal had been faced with the question of whether the owners of a common could stop the defendant driving double-decker buses along a track though a wooded common. The court granted an injunction, holding that a right of way could not be established by twenty years' uninterrupted use, because section 193(4) made it a criminal offence to drive on a common to which the section applied. Whilst this decision preserved the amenity of a common, it resulted in residents of other commons being held to ransom as they found that they had no right to drive over the commons to access their homes. In order to get such a right, they had to pay. Section 68 of the Countryside and Rights of Way Act 2000 came to the rescue to some extent by allowing a right of way to be registered, but it had to be paid for (albeit at a lower rate than that demanded by the some of the companies). The House of Lords has now made section 68 redundant by its decision. Lord Scott, who gave the main speech, admitted that it was a question of public policy but he was able to distinguish most of the previous case law on the grounds that the criminal offence created by section 193(4) was rather unusual, in that it could be condoned by the owner of the common giving lawful authority. The House of Lords did not, however, deal with the consequences of its decision for those who had already paid for a right of way. There is presumably no refund for them!

8.2 McAdams Homes Ltd v Robinson

[2004] EWCA Civ 214; (2004) 101(10) LSG 30

The facts

The claimant owned land on which there was a disused bakery. This had an easement of drainage to the public sewer through pipes used in common with the defendant's adjoining house. The bakery was redeveloped as two separate four-bedroom dwellings and the drainage system was retained. The defendant suffered occasional backflow of material from the public sewer at times of high rainfall and decided to block the drainage used by the two new houses. The claimant had to build alternative drainage connections and claimed the cost of this as damages from the defendant. The defendant claimed that the easement of drainage had been radically varied and was no longer usable in the same manner as beforehand.

The decision:

The Court of Appeal held that the intensification of user amounted to such a radical change that the defendant was entitled to block the use and leave the new development to make its own alternative arrangements.

Comment:

This was a borderline case and another judge might have come to a different decision. It will be a question of degree in each case.

8.3   Hotchkin v McDonald

[2004] EWCA Civ 519; [2004] 18 EG 100 (CS)

The facts:

The defendant owned a house which had enjoyed the benefit of a right of way along a roadway running over adjoining land owned by the claimant. The right of way had been granted in a conveyance to the defendant's predecessors in title in 1965 and had been for all purposes in connection with the use of the house as authorised by a restrictive covenant which had limited the use of the house to office use and for purposes ancillary thereto. The defendant had made an application to the Lands Tribunal under section 84(1) of the Law of Property Act 1925, seeking to discharge or modify the restrictive covenant so as to allow the house to be used for holiday lettings and as a health and fitness centre. The claimant sought a declaration that the right of way could only have been exercised for the purposes as originally authorised in the conveyance, notwithstanding any modification or discharge of the restrictive covenant that the Lands Tribunal might have made. The trial judge made a declaration that the defendant had been entitled to use the right of way for such purposes as were permitted following any modification or discharge of use that may have been made by the Lands Tribunal, and the claimant now appealed.

The decision:

The appeal was dismissed. The language of the conveyance made an express link between the use of the right of way to the house and the use of the house itself. The restriction on the use of the house contained in the conveyance had always been subject to a modification or discharge under section 84 of the 1925 Act, the jurisdiction of which could not have been ousted. That had been a relevant circumstance when the conveyance had been granted. In those circumstances, it would have been unreasonable to have said that the user of the house would have expected to modify or discharge a restriction upon the use of the house without a corresponding change to the right of way.

Comment:

This case illustrates the dangers of linking the scope of a right of way to a restrictive covenant. If the covenant is modified by the Lands Tribunal, the scope of the right of way could also change. To prevent this, the extent of the right of way should be expressly set out in the deed of grant.

8.4 Perlman v Rayden

[2004] EWHC 2192; [2004] 43 EG 142 (CS)

The facts:

The parties owned neighbouring properties, numbered 6A and 6 respectively. A road serving the properties ran along the front elevation of No. 6. The road formed part of the title to No. 6A. The owners of No. 6 had rights of way over it 'for all purposes connected with the existing use of the property as a private dwellinghouse'. The owner of No. 6 covenanted not to park on the road or obstruct it in any way. The owner of No. 6A had a right to enter No. 6 in order to carry out repairs to his property. The rights set out in the transfer of No. 6 were subject to a proviso that the rights were not to be exercised by a person if and so long as he was in material breach of his obligations under the transfer. The defendant had altered and extended No. 6, and parts of the alterations overhung the road. An extension (later demolished) had been constructed in excess of planning permission and with its flank wall abutting the boundary wall with No. 6. The front door and windows of the front elevation of No. 6 had been repositioned. The claimant submitted that use of the road to carry out the building works was unlawful and gave rise to a liability in damages for trespass; the altered features which overhung the road were a trespass for which damages were payable or which had to be removed, as did features whose installation had involved an unlawful use of the road; the right of access to No. 6 did not permit the position of the front door to be moved; a gap for repairing purposes had to be left between No. 6A and any new extension to No. 6; the proviso suspended the defendant's rights while they were unlawfully using the road; he had not consented to the trespasses to the road and was not estopped from complaining about them; and he was entitled to aggravated damages for the mental distress he had suffered which had been increased by the defendant's conduct in constructing the extension.

The decision:

The claimant did have the right to object to any trespass on the road (but not to deliveries effected by the road) to carry out the work. However, he had no right to object to any physical alterations or additions to the property that did not overhang the road. The court conducted a comprehensive review of the authorities, and of the physical features of the particular site in question, and concluded that the grantor of the right of way had intended the grantee to enjoy the widest rights of vehicular and pedestrian access at every point along the road, as opposed to access to a particular point. The claimant had consented to the majority of the work, because he did not raise any objections until construction was well advanced, and could not ask for its removal now. It would be disproportionate to require the removal of any of the remaining alterations because the defendant had made minimal use of the right of way and the changes had not had any adverse effect on the servient land. The claimant was awarded damages instead.

Comment:

It was not appropriate to award an injunction for the removal of any alterations and additions that had resulted from the trespass.

8.5   Sweet v Sommer

[2004] EWHC 1504; [2004] 4 All ER 288 (Note)

The facts:

The applicants sought a declaration that they had a vehicular right of way across land belonging to the defendants. In a 1988 conveyance, the previous owner of the properties had purported to grant vehicular and non-vehicular rights of way when, in fact, he had no power to do so. The effect of the defective transfer was to leave the applicants' property landlocked, except to the extent that it was theoretically possible to demolish a workshop on neighbouring land which would have allowed for access to the property. An issue for determination arose as to whether the circumstances surrounding the transfer were such as to impliedly reserve as a matter of necessity a vehicular right of way.

The decision:

The applicants were entitled to declarations as to their rights of way. Where access to retained land was only available either over the property granted or by destruction of a physical barrier, the continued existence of which was obviously contemplated by the parties, it was consistent with the doctrine to say that a way over the property granted was impliedly reserved as a matter of necessity. A way of necessity could be implied for purposes contemplated at the date of grant but not yet implemented. The circumstances were such that it was obvious from the nature of the house and the circumstances surrounding the grant that a vehicular way was treated as necessary as the house was not useable without it. Therefore, the transfer created, by implied reservation, a vehicular right of way which was a legal easement.

Comment:

This interesting decision confirms that the fact that it may be possible to demolish a physical obstruction will not prevent premises from being landlocked for the purposes of claiming the benefit of an easement of necessity. It also confirms that easements of necessity are not necessarily restricted to pedestrian rights of way.

9   *HUMAN RIGHTS*

9.1   Ghaidan v Godin-Mendoza

[2004] UKHL 30; [2004] 2 AC 557

The facts:

This appeal concerned the survivorship rights of cohabiting same-sex couples in respect of statutory tenancies. The focus of the appeal was the interpretation of Schedule 1, paragraph 2 of the Rent Act 1977, which provides for the succession rights of surviving spouses and those who live together as husband and wife. In *Fitzpatrick v Sterling Housing Association Ltd* ([2001] 1 AC 27), it was held this paragraph did not apply to cohabiting same-sex couples. In the present case, a landlord appealed against the decision that the respondent was entitled to succeed to a tenancy of a flat as a statutory tenant under paragraph 2. The respondent lived with another man who was the tenant of a flat in London.

When the tenant died, the landlord claimed possession. A county court judge held that the respondent did not succeed to the tenancy of the flat as a surviving spouse under paragraph 2, but that he was entitled to an assured tenancy by succession as a member of the original tenant's family under Schedule 1, paragraph 3(1). The respondent appealed and the Court of Appeal held that he was entitled to succeed to a tenancy of the flat as a statutory tenant under paragraph 2. The issue for determination by the House of Lords was how paragraph 2 should be interpreted in the light of the Human Rights Act 1998.

The decision:

Paragraph 2 violated the 1998 Act. There was no justification for the difference in the treatment of heterosexual and same-sex couples. Paragraph 2 was to be interpreted to comply with the 1998 Act in order to eliminate the difference in treatment. Such an interpretation was consistent with the underlying social policy of providing security of tenure.

10 LEASEHOLD COVENANTS

10.1 Norfolk Capital Group Ltd v Cadogan Estates Ltd

[2004] EWHC 384; [2004] 1 WLR 1458

The facts:

The tenant held a 65-year lease of a hotel which contained a covenant prohibiting exterior alterations. The tenant gave notice under section 3(1) of the Landlord and Tenant Act 1927 that it intended to install air-conditioning. The landlord issued a counter-notice that it would carry out the work in return for a rent increase. The tenant preferred to do the work itself and the parties were unable to agree on the amount of the rent increase. The tenant then sought to assign the lease, but the draft licence to assign prepared by the landlord included a clause requiring any potential assignee to agree to the landlord carrying out the works and to the rent increase. The tenant withdrew the improvements notice and brought proceedings seeking a declaration that the landlord was not entitled to carry out the improvements unilaterally.

The decision:

Section 3(1) allowed a court to refuse a certificate authorising the work and, without the certificate, the landlord could not carry out the work. There was no reason to make the tenant accept an improvement carried out by the landlord if it no longer wanted to continue with the improvement. The fact that the landlord had incurred costs in making the offer to carry out the improvement did not matter.

Comment:

Part I of the Landlord and Tenant Act 1927 contains a complex procedure for a tenant to follow if it wants to carry out works which might otherwise be prohibited under the lease. It is of real use where the tenant is facing an absolute bar in the lease against works that it wishes carry out, and section 9 of the Act prevents a landlord and tenant from contracting out of Part I.

10.2 Rother District Investments Ltd v Corke

[2004] EWHC 14; [2004] 2 P & CR 17

The facts:

The claimant was the registered proprietor of the freehold interest in the property. It subsequently purchased the registered headlease, subject to an unregistered underlease in favour of the defendants. The transfer of the headlease was not registered and so the legal title did not pass to the claimant. The defendants ceased to occupy the property, and the underlease became liable to forfeiture for various breaches of covenant. The claimant purported to peaceably re-enter and to forfeit the underlease. It then granted a new underlease to a third party. The claimant then issued proceedings against the defendants for money it was owed, relying upon section 141 of the Law of Property Act 1925 which provides that the right to the arrears passed only if the underlease was subsisting at the date when the legal title to the headlease vested in the claimant.

The decision:

The High Court decided that the acts of the claimant in forfeiting the underlease were effective, as it was possible to presume that the claimant had the authority of the transferor of the headlease, who held the legal title as a bare trustee for the claimant. The claimant had acted as if it had the legal title and could not take advantage of its own wrong to establish a claim to the arrears. The claimant had raised an estoppel which precluded it from denying that it had forfeited the underlease, and the defendants had been entitled to accept that forfeiture, and what had been forfeiture by estoppel, was 'fed' on registration of the headlease.

Comment:

It would have been preferable for the claimant to have taken an express assignment of the right to the arrears, rather than rely upon section 141.

10.3 Mount Cook Land Ltd v Media Business Centre Ltd

[2004] EWHC 346; [2004] 2 P & CR 25

The facts:

In July 2001, the landlord implemented the rent review due on 28 March 2001. An independent expert was appointed. The landlord later became aware that the tenant had breached the alienation covenant and so it served a section 146 notice and, in May 2003, issued forfeiture proceedings. The tenant applied for relief. The expert then set a rent which was higher than anticipated. The landlord discontinued the forfeiture proceedings in December 2003 and claimed the arrears of increased rent backdated to the rent review date. The tenant contended that the lease had been brought to an end on the issue of the forfeiture proceedings.

The decision:

The effect of the discontinuance was to restore the lease. The court was unable to see any valid distinction between circumstances where there was a unilateral discontinuance and circumstances in which the forfeiture claim was dismissed, compromised or in which relief was granted.

Comment:

Where a landlord carries out a peaceable re-entry, it is clear that forfeiture occurs at the moment of re-entry. Where court proceedings are used instead, forfeiture does not occur until the court makes an order for possession. In the meantime, there is a 'twilight period' until the outcome of the proceedings is known. If they are successful, forfeiture takes place with retrospective effect as at the date of service of the proceedings. If they are unsuccessful, withdrawn or compromised, the lease is treated as if it had never been brought to an end. A landlord must be conscious, however, that it may not be possible to discontinue a forfeiture claim in circumstances where the tenant has accepted the right of the landlord to forfeit.

10.4 Iqbal v Thakrar

[2004] EWCA Civ 592; [2004] 36 EG 122

The facts:

The premises consisted of the ground floor of a building of which the landlord owned the top floor as well as the reversion to the tenant's lease. The designated planning use for the premises was for the sale of hot food for consumption on or off the premises. The lease contained a covenant requiring the landlord's consent before structural alterations or additions could be made, such consent not to be unreasonably withheld. The tenant wanted to convert the premises to a restaurant and submitted architect's plans to the landlord, identifying various structural features and load-bearing walls which required checking before work commenced. The landlord refused consent, and so the tenant applied for a declaration that consent had been unreasonably refused. The judge granted the application, holding that the proposed alterations did not pose a threat to the structure and that the real reason for refusing consent was a belief that a restaurant would affect the rental value of the property above. On appeal, the landlord argued that the judge had taken the wrong approach to the test of reasonableness and had failed to give adequate weight to the issue of the building's structural integrity.

The decision:

The appeal was allowed. Consent had been reasonably withheld in the circumstances. The landlord was entitled to seek to protect the structural integrity of the building, and it was for the tenant to show that refusal of consent was unreasonable. It was necessary to establish the real reason for refusing consent before determining, on an objective basis, whether it was unreasonable or not. Alterations to a load-bearing wall could have a detrimental effect on the property, but the plans did not set out what would be done with any such walls. Therefore, the landlord had not been given a full picture on which to decide whether consent should be given, and it was reasonable for him to doubt the viability of the planned alterations.

Comment:

The court applied the principles in *International Drilling Fluids Ltd v*

Louisville Investments (Uxbridge) Ltd ([1986] Ch 513) for consideration when asking if consent to an assignment had been unreasonably withheld. It said that the relevant considerations that a court should consider were that:

a) the purpose of consent was to protect the landlord from alterations that would damage his interest;

b) the landlord was not entitled to refuse consent on a ground that had nothing to do with the value of the property;

c) the onus was on the tenant to prove that the landlord had unreasonably withheld consent to the proposals which he had made, and the tenant was obliged to make the proposals sufficiently clear so that the landlord could decide whether such alterations or additions should be allowed;

d) it was not necessary for the landlord to establish that he had reasonably withheld consent;

e) it might be reasonable for the landlord to refuse consent to a proposed use even if that use was not expressly forbidden by the lease;

f) a landlord should only be expected to consider his own interests except where it would be disproportionate to do so;

g) consent could not be refused on grounds of pecuniary loss alone; and

h) in each case it would be a question of fact whether the landlord, having regard to the actual reason that had impelled him to withhold consent, had acted unreasonably.

10.5 Sergeant v Macepark (Whittlebury) Ltd

[2004] EWHC 1333; [2004] 4 All ER 662

The facts:

The landlord owned a leisure complex made up of a golf course, clubhouse, bars and restaurant. It granted a building lease of land within the complex to the tenant who wanted to develop a hotel. The lease permitted that the hotel could also be used as a 'conference centre' and a 'management training centre'. It also contained a covenant by the landlord not to use its retained premises in a way that would adversely affect the permitted use of the hotel, as well as a fully-qualified covenant by the tenant against alterations. The tenant sought consent from the landlord to extend the hotel and the landlord imposed a condition in the licence for alterations that none of the meeting or conference facilities in the extension should be used 'otherwise than for functions and activities which are directly related or connected to management training conferences held at the premises', as the landlord wanted to prevent competition with its own extensive wedding and functions business.

The decision:

The condition was unreasonable. The landlord was entitled to protect itself against perceived competition to its wedding and functions business, but the proposed condition was unreasonable in that it sought to restrict the use of the extension to management training conferences and excluded all other types of conferences. It therefore conflicted with the covenant given by the landlord in the lease.

Comment:

This is the second case on alterations in which the court has applied the principles laid down in *International Drilling Fluids Ltd v Louisville Investments (Uxbridge) Ltd* ([1986] Ch 513).

10.6 Avonridge Property Co Ltd v Mashru

[2004] EWCA Civ 1306; [2005] 1 WLR 236

The facts:

The appellant, the former tenant under a headlease, appealed against an order that it pay damages to the respondent subtenant for breach of the landlord's covenant contained in the subleases to pay rent to the head landlord. Clause 6 of the sublease purported to limit the appellant's liability on the covenant if it disposed of its interest in the property. The appellant had assigned the headlease to a third party which later defaulted on the rent and the head landlord took action. The trial judge ordered the appellant to pay indemnifying damages to the respondent, who submitted that the clause purporting to limit the appellant's liability was void under the Landlord and Tenant (Covenants) Act 1995. It also argued that the appellant had not taken the necessary steps outlined in section 8 of the Act to obtain release from its obligations and was therefore still liable on the covenant. The appellant submitted that the wording of Clause 6 created a personal covenant which was not a covenant 'falling to be complied with by the landlord of premises demised by the tenancy' under the Act.

The decision:

The appeal was dismissed. The covenant was binding on the appellant's successors in title and was therefore a landlord's covenant. The clause purporting to limit the appellant's liability on disposal was void under the Act, as it was a clear attempt to obtain release in advance and was intended to frustrate the provisions of the Act. The appellant was still liable as it had not followed the procedure under section 8 for obtaining release from the covenant.

Comment:

This decision serves as a warning to landlords who must look carefully at the financial standing of their successors in title, as an undertaking to comply with the landlord's covenants in a lease is only as good as the strength of the covenant behind it. A landlord can apply to be released from liability under the landlord covenants in a lease (but not from any personal covenants) by sending the tenant a notice in the prescribed form. This must be sent before the assignment, or within four weeks after the assignment, and must inform the tenant that he is proposing to assign the lease, or that he has already done so, and that he wishes to be released. The landlord will be released, without needing to take any further action, if the tenant does nothing for four weeks or consents in writing to the release of the landlord. If the tenant objects within four weeks of receiving the landlord's notice, the landlord will have to apply to the county court for a release, failing which the landlord will continue to remain liable under the landlord covenants in the lease. There is no guidance in the Act as to the circumstances in which the court can or should make a declaration that it is reasonable for the landlord to be released from liability under a lease.

11 LEASEHOLD ENFRANCHISEMENT

11.1 Earl Cadogan v Strauss

[2004] EWCA Civ 211; [2004] 2 P & CR 16

The facts:

The tenant had separate leases of a house and an adjoining garden, each of 65 years' duration and at low rents, which had commenced in April 1983. In June 1996, he served his landlord with a notice of leaseholder's claim under the Leasehold Reform Act 1967 by which he purported to exercise his right to buy the freeholds of the properties. The landlord sought a declaration that the notice was invalid on the ground that it failed to comply with the relevant statutory requirements. The notice failed to refer to previous leases of the properties which had commenced in 1972 and which were surrendered to enable the grant of the 1983 leases. The landlord argued that the notice should have given particulars of the composite tenancy formed by linking the 1983 leases with the 1972 leases. At the time he served the notice, the tenant was unaware of the 1972 leases. The landlord now appealed against an order declaring that the tenant was entitled to acquire the freehold.

The decision:

The appeal was dismissed. The notice was a valid notice under the Act. Although the information provided by the tenant was incomplete and inaccurate, there had been no failure to provide information as he had made a serious attempt to provide his landlord with all the information of which he was aware at the date of his claim.

Comment:

In this case, the court treated the tenant's omission of information as a mere excusable inaccuracy.

11.2 Lay v Ackerman

[2004] EWCA Civ 184; [2004] L & TR 29

The facts:

The tenants of premises on the Portman Estate served a notice of claim under section 42 of the Leasehold Reform, Housing and Urban Development Act 1993 on their landlord, proposing a new lease of the premises. The landlord's solicitors prepared and served a counter-notice but this wrongly identified the freehold owners of the premises as the Portman Family Collateral Settlements, which was a subsidiary trust. The judge held that the counter-notice was invalid on the basis that the reference to the wrong trustees as landlord had been deliberate on the part of the solicitors. The landlord appealed.

The decision:

The appeal was allowed. The judge had been wrong to hold that 'deliberate' misidentification of the landlord determined the case. Such a test was inconsistent with *Mannai Investment Co Ltd v Eagle Star Life Assurance Co Ltd* ([1997] AC 749), and was not appropriate under the Act. The correct approach on the basis of *Mannai* was to consider whether there was a mistake in the information contained in the notice, as there was here, in respect of the landlord. If there was such a mistake, the court had to consider how, in the light of the mistake, a reasonable person in the position of the recipient would have understood the notice in the circumstances of the particular case, and whether the notice would have been understood as conveying the information required by the relevant statutory provisions. There was no express statutory requirement for the landlord to be named in the counter-notice. Under section 45 it was clear that it had to be the landlord who served the counter-notice. This meant that the notice had to be served with the authority of the landlord, as it had been here. It was implicit in the requirement that the landlord give the notice that the recipient tenant appreciated that it was the landlord who had given the notice.

Comment:

This is another case dealing with the question of whether *Mannai* is relevant where a notice has been served by the wrong person; however, unlike the other cases which dealt with the exercise of break clauses, the notice in this case was a statutory one. The court confirmed that *Mannai* applied to such notices and so the counter-notice had been valid, despite the misdescription of the landlord, because a reasonable person in the position of the tenant could not have been in any doubt that it had been sent by and with the authority of the actual landlord.

11.3 Long Acre Securities Ltd v Karet

[2004] EWHC 442; [2004] 3 WLR 866

The facts:

In this case, the landlord sought to establish the validity of an offer notice which it had served under section 5B of the Landlord and Tenant Act 1987 on flat tenants of a residential estate. The landlord held the underlease of the estate, which comprised at least four separate structures together with a number of appurtenant areas. Those areas had always been managed as part of the single estate and were used in common by the occupiers of the flats. The landlord had decided to sell part of its interest in the underlease by means of public auction, so it had served the offer notice on the tenants. The word 'building' in the notice purported to include all the flats together with the appurtenant areas. One of the tenants challenged the validity of the notice on the ground that each structure was required by the Act to be the subject of a separate notice.

The facts:

The word 'building' in the Act meant either a single building or one or more buildings where the occupants of qualifying flats in each of those buildings shared the use of the same appurtenant premises. As a matter of pure construction, a notice appeared to be rendered invalid if it dealt with a transaction encompassing more than one building. However, it was necessary to have regard to the purpose of the legislation, namely to give tenants the right to acquire their landlord's reversion, and to provide a workable procedure to achieve that purpose. Parliament could not be taken to have intended that appurtenant areas would have to be split in order to satisfy the Act with the result that any alternative construction would make the Act unworkable. Accordingly, the notice was valid.

51

Comment:

The circumstances where separate notices have to be served for each part of a complex, or where a single notice is sufficient, are not defined. It appears from this case that although the preference is for separate notices to be served for each separate building, where a complex is so interconnected as to render the only realistic treatment to be one where subdivision is avoided, then a series of separate structures can be treated as a 'building'.

11.4 Slamon v Planchon

[2004] EWCA Civ 799; [2004] 4 All ER 407

The facts:

This appeal involved the resident landlord exception to collective enfranchisement in the Leasehold Reform, Housing and Urban Development Act 1993. The particular issue which had to be determined was whether the freeholder had an adequate interest. Her mother was the occupier of one of the three flats in the building, and the freeholder relied on her mother's occupation, together with her own interest in the freehold of the house over a long period stretching back to before the time of its conversion into flats.

The decision:

The Act required the 'same person' to have owned the freehold of the premises since before the conversion. There had to be continuity on the part of the freeholder or, if the freehold was held on trust, on the part of the person having an interest under the trust. In this particular case, there was no continuity of either kind. The legislation was expropriatory. There was no indication that the interests could be mixed with each other to result in a continuous whole. It could only be assumed from the statutory language that Parliament intended that, at the relevant date, the same person should either own the freehold from before the conversion, or be a beneficiary under the same trust since before the conversion.

Comment:

This decision confirms that where a landlord does not have a continuous interest in the property, for example where he has for part of the time held the property as a freeholder and for part of the time as a beneficiary under a trust, this will not be sufficient to satisfy the resident landlord requirement under the 1993 Act.

11.5 Earl Cadogan v Search Guarantees plc

[2004] EWCA Civ 969; [2004] 1 WLR 2768

The facts:

The appellant held a lease of some flats that it had sublet on short-term tenancies. It was accepted that the appellant was the 'qualifying tenant' for the purposes of the Leasehold Reform, Housing and Urban Development Act 1993 and that, by virtue of the headlease, it was also the tenant of the house in which the flats were situated. The court at first instance had found that the appellant, being a company, was not entitled to enfranchise because it did not meet the requirements of section 1(1ZB) of the Leasehold Reform Act 1967. The appellant submitted that the court had wrongly construed this provision, and that its clear purpose was to resolve potential conflicts between different tenants at different levels in the chain by dealing with who should have the right to enfranchise when the tenant of the house was a different person from the tenant of a flat forming part of the house. Although the respondents conceded that that might be the primary purpose of the provision, they maintained that such a construction was only illustrative of its application and not definitive of its full scope. The appellant appealed against a declaration that it was not entitled to enfranchise.

The decision:

The appeal was allowed. One of the purposes of the changes to the 1967 Act, effected by the Commonhold and Leasehold Reform Act 2002, was to change the law so as to allow companies to obtain enfranchisement. The logical reason for retaining the residence requirement in the special circumstances of section 1(1ZB) was to resolve which of two people should have the right to seek enfranchisement. If the respondent's view was followed, it would mean that parties in the same situation as the appellant could not obtain enfranchisement of their interest, but could still obtain extension of each of the leases for all of the individual flats of which they were the qualifying tenant. That would produce the bizarre result of their being able to have longer leases for the flats than they would have for the common parts. Accordingly, section 1(1ZB) did not apply to the appellant and did not prevent it from obtaining enfranchisement.

Comment:

The decision in this case will not allow head tenants to bring a claim for the freehold of a house where there are qualifying tenants of flats within the house. If the head-tenant is a different person to the qualifying tenants for lease extension, section 1(1ZB) will clearly apply, and those with long leasehold interests will be protected against enfranchisement by a non-resident landlord under the 1967 Act, unless of course they satisfy the residency test. However, they will, potentially, still have the right to collective enfranchisement under the 1993 Act.

11.6 Fattal v John Lyon Free Grammar School Governors

[2004] EWCA Civ 1530; [2005] 1 All ER 466

The facts:

The property was originally a four-bedroom house with no bathroom or garage. After the tenant had carried out extensive works, the property had seven bedrooms and seven bathrooms, a swimming pool complex and two garages. The tenant had served notice to acquire the freehold under the Leasehold Reform Act 1967. The Lands Tribunal had determined the price to be paid but it had further ascertained lower alternative amounts that it would have determined if it had come to a different decision on points of law put forward by the tenant in relation to valuation under section 9(1A)(d) of the 1967 Act. The tenant appealed and submitted that development potential (including, in particular, the value of any planning permission) was to be left out of account in valuing the property; the value of the property should be assessed by taking its improved value and then deducting the value of tenant's improvements and, if the property was valued on the basis that the improvements had never been carried out, then the planning permissions that enabled them to be carried out should also be disregarded.

The decision:

The appeal was dismissed. The assumption in section 9(1A)(d) (that the price was to be diminished by the extent to which the value of the house and premises had been increased by any improvement carried out by the tenant) did not imply that the value of the potential for improvement had to be excluded from the valuation of the unimproved house. Assumption (d) required a calculation of the amount of the increase in value caused by the improvements. That involved a valuation of the property as it would have been on the valuation date if it had not been improved. Any potential for improvement would be included in the achieved sale prices of unimproved properties, so that a valuation of an unimproved house and premises would include the value of any such potential. Therefore, an increase in value caused by an actual improvement had to be calculated as an excess over the unimproved valuation, including the value of the potential for improvement, notwithstanding that the potential was merged in or absorbed by the actual improvement. Section 9(1A)(d) did not restrict the valuer in his analysis to a 'top down' basis of valuation, as the tenant contended, thus preventing him from considering unimproved comparables. Assumption (d) simply required that the price be diminished by the extent stated. It did not impose any requirement that the house and premises should be valued either from the top down or from the bottom up. The method adopted was a matter of valuation, not of law. The method adopted (of valuing the property as if it had never been improved at all) was the standard method adopted by the Lands Tribunal. Assuming that the issue of the planning permissions was a separate point from the first point, the tenant's submission failed. An improvement was a physical concept. It was the increase in value caused by the physical works that had to be subtracted and the existence or availability of planning permission was not part of those works.

Comment:

In this case, the tenant had made improvements that increased the value of the house and, in calculating the price, it was necessary to look at the value of the property with the improvements and the value without them and to calculate the difference. The problem was that the valuation of the unimproved property would include an element of value arising from the potential for improvement and this could not be disregarded.

11.7 7 Strathay Gardens Ltd v Pointstar Shipping & Finance Ltd

[2004] EWCA Civ 1669; [2005] 07 EG 144

The facts:

The landlord appealed against an order that its counter-notice served in response to a notice of collective enfranchisement was invalid and the respondent, as the tenants' nominee purchaser, was entitled to acquire the freehold and leasehold interests in the premises. The tenants had served a notice of collective enfranchisement. The landlord served a counter-notice which did not state, as required by Regulation 4 of the Leasehold Reform (Collective Enfranchisement) (Counter-notices) (England) Regulations 2002, whether the premises were in the area of a scheme approved as an estate management scheme. The premises were not in such an area and the counter-notice should, therefore, have included a negative statement. The judge found that the requirement in Regulation 4 was mandatory and the counter-notice was therefore invalid. The landlord submitted that the requirement was directory and therefore failure to comply with it did not invalidate the notice.

The decision:

The appeal was allowed. Regulation 4 was not to be treated as if it formed part of statutory requirements. It was a self-standing requirement. Neither the Regulations nor the Leasehold Reform, Housing and Urban Development Act 1993 expressly stated that a notice was not valid unless it complied with the Act or Regulations. The position was left to the courts to determine as a matter of interpretation. The Regulations clearly did not contain essential machinery. Regulation 4 contained two mutually exclusive separate requirements – in certain circumstances it required a negative statement and in other circumstances it required a positive statement. A mere negative statement could not have been intended to be mandatory. There could be no possible prejudice to the tenants or their nominee purchaser if that information was excluded. Further, there was no suggestion in the discussion paper preceding the Regulations that there could be any benefit to tenants in requiring a negative statement where the premises were not subject to an estate management scheme. Therefore, the requirement in Regulation 4 for a negative statement was not mandatory.

Comment:

This is a straightforward decision. The effect of non-compliance with a particular statutory requirement depends on the particular statutory scheme; this decision involved a consideration of the statutory requirement and the reasons for it.

12   MISREPRESENTATION

12.1 Pankhania v Hackney London Borough Council

[2004] EWHC 323; [2004] 1 EGLR 135

The facts:

The claimant was a property developer who was claiming damages from the defendant for negligent misrepresentation. After the claimant had bought a car park and a factory from the local authority for £3,925,000 at auction, it transpired that a third party occupied the car park under a business tenancy protected by Part II of the Landlord and Tenant Act 1954 and not under a licence as had been represented by the defendant. The claimant eventually obtained possession of the car park after having paid £78,931 to the occupier. The claimant argued that the damages should be assessed as the difference between the price he had actually paid for the properties and their true value at the date of purchase, and that this amounted to approximately £750,000. The defendant argued that the claimant had failed to mitigate his loss, and could therefore only claim the amount he would have had to pay to the occupier if he had acted reasonably, which was £45,000.

The decision:

The damages to be awarded for misrepresentation under section 2(1) of the Misrepresentation Act 1967 were the same as for fraudulent misrepresentation. The normal measure of damages was subject to the principle that a claimant was entitled to reparation for all actual damage he had sustained arising from the transaction. The claimant had not been shown to have acted unreasonably in failing to obtain possession sooner, and on a fair valuation of the properties as at the date of auction and subject to the occupier's tenancy, the appropriate award was £500,000.

Comment:

The normal measure for damages in these types of cases is the difference between the price actually paid for the properties and their true value at the date of purchase.

12.2 Sykes v Taylor-Rose

[2004] EWCA Civ 299; [2004] 2 P & CR 30

The facts:

In March 1999, the seller had received an anonymous note telling him that a horrific murder had been committed in his house in the early 1980s. He contacted his solicitor who told him that when he had bought his house, the seller had not been obliged to disclose the history of the house and that he, in turn, would be under no such obligation should he sell it. Some 18 months later the seller put the house on the market and accepted an offer of £83,000. As part of the normal enquiries before contract, the seller was sent a 'Seller's Property Information Form'. Question 13 of that form asked 'Is there any other information which you think the buyer may have a right to know'. Acting on his solicitor's advice, he said 'no'. The transfer was completed and the buyer moved into the property in December 2000. In July 2001, he watched a television documentary which detailed the events surrounding the murder at the property. The programme inferred that some of the victim's body parts may still have been hidden in the house. The buyer was horrified and moved out of the house. The property was put up for sale and the circumstances of the murder were disclosed to prospective buyers. Six months later, the house was sold for £75,000 although its market value without the history was, according to the buyer, around £100,000. The buyer maintained that the seller's answer to Question 13 amounted to a misrepresentation and/or a negligent misstatement which gave rise to a claim for damages. The buyer now appealed against the dismissal of his claim.

The decision:

The appeal was dismissed. Question 13 was concerned with information which the buyer might have had a right to know. There was nothing in its wording to alert the seller to the suggestion that the answer would imply that he had reasonable grounds for the answer. The question was subjective and had to be answered honestly. As the question only required an honest answer, there could have been no breach of any duty to answer the question on a reasonable basis. Further, given that the seller had acted on his solicitor's advice, it could not be said that he had acted negligently.

Comment:

This case highlights that, when considering a seller's liability for non-disclosure, a distinction must be made between liability under the exception to the caveat emptor rule and liability for misrepresentation. It also illustrates that the duty of disclosure will depend on whether the question is directed to factual matters, matters of knowledge or matters of opinion. A question as to matters of opinion will not, in the absence of other provisions, require more than an honest view. The question on the Seller's Property Information Form which was at the centre of this case has not appeared on the form for some time, so the issue of the extent of the obligation of disclosure is no longer relevant. However, a conveyancer might ask a specific additional question about crimes committed at the property and a seller who refuses to answer such a question would make it look like they have something to hide.

13 MORTGAGES

13.1 Yorkshire Bank plc v Tinsley

[2004] EWCA Civ 816; [2004] 3 All ER 463

The facts:

In 1988 the appellant's husband had bought some business units with the aid of a mortgage that was secured on the units and the jointly owned matrimonial home. In 1991 that mortgage was replaced by a new mortgage to the respondent. As part of divorce proceedings in 1994, it was arranged that the matrimonial home would be exchanged for a flat in the appellant's sole name and the proceeds used to discharge the mortgage. However, the respondent insisted on a substitute charge on the flat to secure the husband's business debts as a condition of releasing the charge over the matrimonial home. The husband failed to discharge the mortgage and the respondent sought a possession order against the appellant. The judge decided that the 1988 and 1991 mortgages were voidable as against the first lender for undue influence and that, since the respondent had constructive notice of that undue influence, they were voidable as against it as well. However, the judge concluded that this did not affect the validity of the 1994 mortgage and granted a possession order. The appellant appealed and submitted that any substitution for the voidable charges was also voidable unless she, knowing that the charge was voidable, chose to affirm it or by her conduct led the respondent to alter its position.

The decision:

The appeal was allowed. If a mortgage or guarantee was voidable for undue influence as against a husband and a bank, a replacement mortgage, even if undue influence was not operative at the time of such replacement, would itself be voidable, at any rate if the replacement mortgage was taken out as a condition of discharging an earlier voidable mortgage. That should be the case even if there was a new contract rather than a mere variation of an old contract. Where the replacement mortgage was made with the same lender, there was no reason why the constructive notice should be deemed to have disappeared when the earlier mortgage was discharged. The respondent had insisted on the substitute mortgage and thereby inseparably connected the 1994 mortgage with the 1998 and 1991 mortgages and, since it was fixed with constructive notice of the invalidity of those mortgages, it was also fixed with notice of the comparable invalidity of the 1994 mortgage.

Comment:

This is an important decision which confirms that a lender granting a substitute mortgage must not only make sure that the Etridge guidelines are followed in relation to the new mortgage but must also verify that the earlier mortgage it granted is not voidable. A lender should know from its records whether or not it protected itself in respect of the earlier mortgage, but if it cannot confirm this, then it should still be able to protect itself by making sure that the wife receives independent legal advice on the discharge of the earlier mortgage and the grant of the new mortgage.

13.2 Michael v Miller

[2004] EWCA Civ 282; [2004] 2 EGLR 151

The facts:

The claimants appealed against the judge's decision that the defendant had not acted in breach of duty on the sale of an estate in Gloucestershire, and the defendant cross-appealed against the decision that he was in breach of duty in not selling certain plants on the land separately. The claimants bought the estate from the defendant in 1993. They paid a 10% deposit and the balance of the purchase price was left outstanding as a loan secured by a legal charge over the whole estate. The claimant's ownership of the estate was a commercial failure and they were unable to repay the loan. In 1997 the defendant obtained a possession order and instructed a valuer to sell the estate. The claimants had planted a large quantity of lavender on the estate which they believed had a significant market value. The estate was sold for £1,625,000 after a last-minute reduction of £25,000. The claimants claimed that the defendant had breached its duty as mortgagee to take reasonable care to obtain the best price. The judge heard expert valuation evidence and concluded that the market value of the estate at the date of sale was £1,750,000 but that an acceptable range for valuations was from £1,600,000 to £1,900,000. The agent had not acted negligently, but the defendant had breached his duty as mortgagee by agreeing the last-minute reduction and in not marketing the lavender plants separately since they appeared to have some commercial value.

The decision:

The appeal was dismissed. Subject to any restrictions in the mortgage deed, it was for a mortgagee to decide how a sale should be advertised and for how long a property should be left on the market. Such decisions inevitably involved an exercise of informed judgment. There was no absolute duty to advertise widely. A mortgagee would not breach his duty to a mortgagor if, in the exercise of the power of sale, he exercised his judgment reasonably and, to the extent that that judgment involved assessing market value, the mortgagee would have acted reasonably if his assessment fell within an acceptable margin of error. In so far as the exercise of a mortgagee's power of sale called for the exercise of informed judgment, the use of a margin of error had to be available to courts as a means of assessing whether a mortgagee had failed to exercise that judgment reasonably.

Comment:

In this particular case, the judge had taken the unsatisfactory course of first deciding what was the market value and then asking himself whether the mortgagee was negligent in achieving a price substantially less. As the property had been exposed to the market and a number of genuine offers had been received, the more logical approach was to start by considering the steps which the mortgagee had taken to sell the property and then consider whether it had acted reasonably in accepting the buyer's offer.

14 PLANNING

14.1 Eastleigh Borough Council v First Secretary of State

[2004] EWHC 1408; [2004] 24 EG 149 (CS)

The facts:

A supermarket applied for a lawful development certificate to increase its sales floor space by the conversion of existing storage space or the installation of a mezzanine floor. The supermarket was originally built with 50,000 square feet of selling space and, currently, forty years after the original development, the sales area was 83,300 square feet. None of the consents issued for the series of expansions that had taken place imposed any express condition limiting the level of retail floor space. The planning authority claimed that that proposal would amount to a material change of use by reason of intensification. This fell outside the rights under the Town and Country Planning (Use Classes) Order 1987 which authorised other uses so long as they fell within the same class. The operator succeeded in its planning appeal and the planning authority applied to have the decision quashed.

The decision:

Whilst intensification is a matter which does normally require a planning consent (as the degree of change amounts to development), where the use remains in the same use class as beforehand, no development is deemed to take place. Thus the change was lawful.

Comment:

This case confirmed that an intensification of use following the construction of a mezzanine floor in a supermarket did not constitute a material change of use of the premises as the intensified use would fall within the same use class as the existing use. Changes to be introduced by the government will mean that, in future, planning permission will be needed before a mezzanine floor can be installed.

15 PROFESSIONAL NEGLIGENCE

15.1 Hilton v Barker Booth & Eastwood (A Firm)

[2005] UKHL 8; [2005] 1 All ER 651

The facts:

The appellant appealed against a decision dismissing his claim for damages against the respondents, a firm of solicitors for breach of their contractual duty. The appellant had instructed the firm to act as his solicitors in respect of his property development business. The appellant had agreed to purchase a development site, build flats on it and sell the developed property to another client of the firm. The firm did not disclose to the appellant that they had a conflict of interest because they were lending their client the deposit for the purchase from the appellant, nor did they disclose to the appellant their knowledge that their client had been declared bankrupt and was a convicted fraudster. The firm's client failed to complete the transaction and the property was sold by the bank as mortgagee. The appellant's business collapsed. The judge found that if the appellant had been informed of the firm's client's antecedents, he would not have become involved in the transaction. The judge held that the firm was in breach of duty but that the breach had caused no loss. The Court of Appeal dismissed the appellant's appeal on the basis that the retainer and duty of disclosure to the appellant were subject to an implied exclusion of information which the firm was obliged to treat as confidential.

The decision:

The firm could not properly act on both sides of the transaction in question and were under a duty to inform the appellant that they could not act for him and that he should seek legal advice from other solicitors. The notion of confidentiality, as generally understood by lawyers, was not really relevant to the issues in the case. It was a solicitor's duty to act in his client's best interests and not to do anything likely to damage his client's interests, so far as that was consistent with the solicitor's professional duty. To disclose discreditable facts about a client, and to do so without the client's informed consent, was likely to be a breach of duty, even if the facts were in the public domain. Disclosure by the firm of their client's past would have been a breach of their duty to him. The Court of Appeal was wrong to hold that the retainer contained an implied exclusion from the duty of disclosure. Such an implied term would not satisfy the well-known tests for implied terms and would have amounted to the appellant agreeing that, because his solicitors had failed in their duty to tell him to take separate advice and had instead proceeded to act for him as well as for their client, in a matter in which they had a financial interest, their duty to him had to be curtailed in order to accommodate their first breach of duty. The notion that one breach of duty should exonerate the firm in respect of a subsequent and more serious breach of duty was contrary to common sense and justice. If a solicitor put himself in a position of having two irreconcilable duties, it was his own fault. If he had a personal interest which conflicted with his duty, he was even more obviously at fault. The firm was not exonerated from liability by the fact that they could not satisfy their duty both to the appellant and to their client.

Comment:

This is an important case and makes it clear that if a solicitor undertakes irreconcilably conflicting duties, it is his own fault and it will be liable to one of its clients. Unfortunately, the House of Lords did not give any guidance on what point a conflict will give rise to an actionable breach. The moral is that the firm should have sent one of its clients elsewhere.

16   RENT REVIEW

16.1 Chancebutton Ltd v Compass Services UK & Ireland Ltd

[2004] EWHC 1293; [2004] 2 EGLR 47

The facts:

The claimant, who held a reversionary interest in office premises, sought a declaration as to the meaning of a rent review clause in the lease. The lease had been granted from 24 June 1982 for a term of 25 years less one day. The unexpired residue of the term created by the lease was vested in the defendant. A rent review date arose on 24 June 2002. Each review date in the lease called for a 'current market rent' which was defined as that which could be expected to be obtained if the premises were being granted for a term 'equal to the term originally granted under this lease'. The claimant submitted that the hypothetical term being granted was the period remaining of the 25 years less one day granted in 1982. The defendant argued that the term was a hypothetical term of 25 years less one day commencing on 24 June 2002.

The decision:

The presumption in favour of reality and natural meaning of the language used in the lease favoured the construction put forward by the claimant. A term of 25 years from 24 June 2002 would not be 'equal to the term originally granted' and so the reference should be construed so as to mean the unexpired residue of the original term.

Comment:

In the current market, this decision will result in a significantly higher rent as 25-year leases attract a discount over, say, a lease granted for 10 or 15 years. If the unexpired residue is too short it can be onerous. A tenant might then be able to claim successfully that he should have a discount to offset high hypothetical fit-out costs.

16.2 St George's Investment Co v Gemini Consulting Ltd

[2004] EWHC 2353; [2005] 01 EG 96

The facts:

The claimant applied for the remission of an arbitration award for reconsideration under section 68 of the Arbitration Act 1996, on the ground that a serious irregularity had occurred in the course of the proceedings before the arbitrator. The landlord had granted an underlease of the lower ground floor of an office building to the defendant. The parties had failed to agree on the level of the reviewed rent payable in December 2001, so it was referred to an arbitrator. Written representations were made by the parties to the arbitrator through their expert valuers. The third floor of the premises was also demised to the tenant by a separate lease on similar terms which had been the subject of a December 2001 rent review. The landlord submitted that the rent of the lower ground floor should be discounted by 30% from the adjusted third floor figure of £55 and the tenant submitted that the rent should be discounted by 65%. The arbitrator used a discount of 40% as the starting point for his rent calculation. He then made a further discount of 9% adjusting for the onerous features of the lease. The landlord submitted that the arbitrator had produced a result which had not been the subject of submission before him and which it had no opportunity to answer by making the additional discount of 9% for the onerous lease terms, thereby departing from the agreed basis upon which the case was put to him. The tenant submitted that there was no serious irregularity because the issue of the onerous lease discounts was in the arena before the arbitrator and that, in any event, no substantial injustice had occurred.

The decision:

It was clear that the arbitrator started with the third floor discount method put forward by the parties. The award in respect of the third floor did not include any discount for onerous lease terms. The onerous lease terms discount was inconsistent with the third floor discount method and involved double counting. It was not a discount which was to be applied in determining the discount between an upper floor and a lower ground floor. The onerous lease terms discount was not in the arena for decision by the arbitrator because the parties had made their representations to the arbitrator on a totally different basis. It appeared that the arbitrator had made his calculation on a basis which was contrary to the agreed assumptions between the parties and which appeared to confuse the two methodologies of valuation. Consequently, there had been a serious irregularity. The irregularity had caused substantial injustice to the landlord and the award was remitted in whole to the arbitrator for reconsideration.

Comment:

It is very difficult to challenge arbitration awards in the courts and few such challenges have succeeded since the Arbitration Act 1996 came into force. This decision is a rare example of a successful challenge to an arbitrator's award.

16.3 Epoch Properties Ltd v British Home Stores (Jersey) Ltd

[2004] 48 EG 134

The facts:

The respondent ran a clothing and household retail store in Jersey. The lease allowed for an independent surveyor to be appointed by the president of the Royal Institute of Chartered Surveyors as an expert to decide the rent review issue. The surveyor had to have relevant experience of assessing 'broadly similar' properties in Jersey unless no such properties existed; in which case, experience of properties in the United Kingdom was acceptable. The respondent applied for a surveyor to be appointed, and the president decided that there were no surveyors with the relevant experience in Jersey and appointed a London-based surveyor. The landlord challenged the appointment, but its application was dismissed by the Royal Court, which held that the appointment had been properly made. The landlord appealed, arguing that the premises had been wrongly identified as a 'variety store' with the result that no surveyors with relevant experience were available in Jersey.

The decision:

The appeal was dismissed. The president had adopted the correct approach, in accordance with industry practice, of first deciding what retail category the premises fell into. The evidence of the tenant's expert pointed clearly towards it being within the 'variety store' category and that evidence was to be preferred. As there were no similar variety stores on Jersey, it was right that an outside expert be appointed. Having followed the required procedure and having taken into account the relevant factors for appointment of the surveyor, the president's decision could not be impugned by the fact that he had then used his discretion to add the additional 'good sense' factor of trying to choose a member of his own panel.

Comment:

This is a novel decision about the validity of the appointment of an expert to determine a rent review. Where the president of the RICS appoints an expert, the appointment must comply with the requirements in the lease, but where this involves the exercise of the president's expertise, all that is necessary is that his decision is not perverse.

17 RESIDENTIAL TENANCIES

17.1 North British Housing Association Ltd v Matthews

[2004] EWCA Civ 1736; [2005] 2 EG 101 (CS)

The facts:

The tenant appealed against the district judge's refusal to adjourn an application for possession brought by the respondent. The tenant was an assured tenant and the respondent had issued possession proceedings on the basis of the tenant's arrears of rent. As at least eight weeks' rent was unpaid at the date of the hearing before the district judge, he had to order possession under Ground 8 of Schedule 2, Part I, of the Housing Act 1988. The tenant was entitled to housing benefit and had been unable to pay the rent because the housing benefit authority had not paid her. The tenant had applied to adjourn the possession proceedings in order to give herself time to obtain money either to meet the arrears, or at least to bring her below the eight-week threshold at which the court was obliged to order possession. She argued that it was in the interests of justice to adjourn the hearing of the claim in order to afford her a defence which she did not have at the date of the first hearing.

The decision:

The appeal was dismissed. In principle, it was not legitimate for the court (before it was satisfied that the landlord was entitled to possession), to order an adjournment designed to achieve a result which the law current at the date of the hearing would not permit. The power to adjourn a hearing date for the purpose of enabling a tenant to reduce the arrears below the Ground 8 threshold could only be exercised in exceptional circumstances. The power was not to be exercised so as to defeat the policy of the Act or the rights which it conferred on landlords. The fact that arrears were attributable to maladministration on the part of the housing benefit authority was not an exceptional circumstance, and the non-receipt of housing benefit could not, of itself, amount to an exceptional circumstance which would justify the exercise of the power to adjourn so as to enable the tenant to defeat the claim. Once the court had expressed the conclusion that the landlord was entitled to possession then, by virtue of section 9(6) of the Act, there was no power to grant an adjournment in any circumstances.

Comment:

This is a harsh decision which makes it clear that an adjournment will only be granted in exceptional circumstances. Whilst the court expressed sympathy for the appellant, it was clear that arrears that are attributable to maladministration on the part of the housing benefit authorities are not an exceptional circumstance. By way of consolation, the court did urge the Housing Corporation to strengthen its advice to registered social landlords to encourage them to liaise closely with housing benefit authorities, before and during any possession proceedings.

18 RESTRICTIVE COVENANTS

18.1 Crest Nicholson Residential (South) Ltd v McAllister

[2004] EWCA Civ 410; [2004] 2 All ER 991

The facts:

Several plots of land had been sold by two brothers operating as a company, by way of conveyances which contained restrictive covenants; first, preventing the use of the property for any purpose other than in connection with a private dwellinghouse or for professional purposes and, secondly, preventing the construction of a dwellinghouse without the prior approval of the seller. The conveyances expressed that the covenants were made with the seller but not its successors. Three of the conveyances contained express words of annexation, whilst three others did not. The appellant entered into a conditional contract to buy land which was subject to these covenants with a view to building five new houses on it. The respondent, who owned neighbouring land, challenged the plans on the basis that she had the benefit of the restrictive covenants. The judge held that the building restriction had become spent on the death of the two brothers or the dissolution of their company. However, he found that the effect of the user restriction was to preclude the appellant from erecting more than one dwellinghouse. The appellant argued that, on a true construction of the relevant conveyances and having regard to the language of section 78 of the Law of Property Act 1925, there was no annexation to land which ceased to be in the ownership of the company or the two brothers.

The decision:

The appeal was allowed. The benefit of the covenants was not annexed to the land owned by the respondent. The effect of the express words of annexation contained in the first three conveyances was to identify the land of the covenantee intended to be benefited for the purposes of section 78(1), in terms that excluded land which was in the ownership of the company at the time of the relevant conveyance but which, thereafter, was sold by the company. The conclusion on annexation precluded the need for findings on the effect of the restrictions.

Comment:

In this case, the Court of Appeal has confirmed that the right to enforce the benefit of a restrictive covenant does not pass to successors in title under section 78 where the land to be benefited by the covenant cannot be identified. Restrictive covenants must be very carefully drafted and, for section 78 to operate, the land which is to benefit must be capable of being identified. Where express words of annexation are used, they must accurately describe the land to benefit.

18.2 Jarvis Homes Ltd v Marshall

[2004] EWCA Civ 839; [2004] 44 EG 154

The facts:

Two adjoining properties were originally owned by the same person. In 1964, one of them was sold and the conveyance contained a restrictive covenant preventing the construction of anything other than a two-storey building on the property and contained the words 'use the same as a private residence only'. Jarvis subsequently purchased the property and wanted to construct a new house on part of the site, along with an access road leading to a further ten new dwellings which it intended to build on land behind the property. Mr and Mrs Marshall argued that the construction and use of the roadway as a means of access to the proposed development was a breach of covenant. However, the judge held that it would not be a breach and the Marshalls appealed.

The decision:

The appeal was allowed. The words used showed that the land was only to be used for a private residence, which did not include the use of part of the site for an access road. The covenant was intended to bind the original owners and their successor in title, including licensees, and be for the benefit of the neighbouring property, which had been built on land retained by the former owner of the site.

Comment:

This decision turned on an interpretation of the words of the covenant, and is another case which illustrates how important it is for the draftsman to carefully consider the extent of the restriction.

18.3 Martin v David Wilson Homes Ltd

[2004] EWCA Civ 1027; [2004] 39 EG 134

The facts:

The defendant appealed against a decision on a preliminary issue arising from the enforcement of a restrictive covenant. A local authority development corporation had sold two plots of land, Plots 2 and 3, each of which was subject to a restrictive covenant designed to prevent the land from being used for any purpose other than as 'a private dwellinghouse'. A dwellinghouse was built on each plot. The defendant acquired a large part of both Plot 2 and 3, not including the existing dwellinghouses, and began the construction of 24 dwellinghouses. The claimant claimed the benefit of the covenants. At a preliminary hearing, the court decided that the indefinite article in the phrase 'a private dwellinghouse' meant that no more than one building on each plot could be used as a dwellinghouse.

The decision:

The appeal was allowed. The presence of the indefinite article 'a' in the covenant restricted the manner of use but not the number of buildings. The schedule to the conveyances containing the covenant referred to 'any buildings', clearly envisaging the possibility that there might be several. The use of the indefinite article in the phrase 'a private dwellinghouse' did not imply singularity.

Comment:

In this case, the Court of Appeal looked at the question of construction from the literal wording, the facts of the case and the case law authority. The covenant referred to 'any buildings' and 'any part of the plot'. In this context 'use as a private dwellinghouse' was a phrase that could apply to the use of several dwellinghouses. The facts indicated that a prestigious development was envisaged with a substantial garden. However, had the intention been that only one dwellinghouse were to be allowed, this should have been reflected in greater detail in the covenant. Despite the ruling in *Crest Nicholson Residential (South) Ltd v McAllister* ([2004] EWCA Civ 410; [2004] 2 All ER 991), the Court of Appeal in this particular case permitted the development.

18.4 Mortimer v Bailey

[2004] EWCA Civ 1514; [2005] 02 EG 102

The facts:

The appellants appealed against the making of a mandatory injunction sought by the respondents requiring them to demolish an extension to their home. The parties were neighbours. The appellants' property was subject to a restrictive covenant that required the respondents' prior written approval of any building works carried out on it. That approval could not be unreasonably withheld. The appellants decided to extend their home and, in February 2003, told the respondents who made it clear that they would not grant approval. The appellants considered that the refusal was unreasonable and, in June 2003, commenced construction. Soon afterwards, the respondents made it clear that if the works did not cease, they would commence proceedings. At the end of July 2003, they applied for an interim injunction seeking to prevent the continuation of the works. The judge refused that application on the basis that there was only a week's worth of works left to complete the extension, saying that if the respondents had made their application in June the position would have been different. Further, he held that if he were wrong on that point, he would have refused to grant the injunction in any event, as damages were an adequate remedy. At the subsequent trial, it was found that the reasons put forward by the respondents justified their withholding of consent. The judge further found that damages would not have been an adequate remedy given that the appellant had ignored the covenant.

The decision:

It was doubtful whether a person who had not sought an interlocutory injunction in the knowledge that a building was being erected, but who had made it clear that he objected to that construction as a breach of covenant, and who subsequently commenced proceedings, was barred from obtaining a final injunction. There could very well be circumstances where a claimant would not be able to risk an interim injunction and the dangers that came with it, namely, undertakings in damages. Accordingly, whilst the issue of delay could be a matter to be taken into account in the overall balance, in the instant case it had not defeated the respondents' claim. In light of the judge's finding that the refusal had not been unreasonable, there was no reason to interfere with the judge's discretion.

Comment:

Where there is doubt about the applicability of a restrictive covenant, a prudent party should have that issue determined before building, otherwise there is a considerable risk that the covenant would be upheld. The appellants had chosen to rely on advice to continue with the construction and, in so doing, they had taken a gamble that it had been unreasonable for the respondent to withhold consent.

19 UNDUE INFLUENCE

19.1 Macklin v Dowsett

[2004] EWCA Civ 904; [2004] 2 EGLR 75

The facts:

The appellant's bungalow had been demolished after being condemned by the local council and he obtained planning permission to build a replacement. In the meantime, he lived in a caravan. He transferred his property to the respondent in return for a life tenancy entitling him to live there rent-free for the rest of his life. One month before the planning permission expired, the respondent laid foundations and entered into an option agreement with the appellant, which provided that he would surrender his life tenancy for a premium of £5,000 if the bungalow was not completed within three years. At the end of the three years, the respondent sought to enforce the option as the appellant had not started the building work. The appellant now appealed against the decision that the option agreement was not affected by undue influence.

The decision:

The appeal was allowed. The appellant had shown a dependency on the respondent, who was in a much stronger position and able to dictate disadvantageous terms to him. The judge had failed to consider whether the option agreement required an explanation as to why the appellant had given the respondent the right to acquire the rent-free life tenancy for only £5,000 and there was no basis for finding that the appellant had obtained any benefit from the agreement.

Comment:

This case applied the principles of undue influence in *Royal Bank of Scotland plc v Etridge (No 2)* ([2001] UKHL 44), to an option agreement. The Court of Appeal focused on the relationship between the parties at the time the option was granted, and the key factor was the financial disparity between the parties' bargaining positions. This was sufficient to establish some relationship of ascendancy and dependency. Unfortunately, the Court of Appeal did not take the opportunity to provide guidance on the steps which a conveyancer should take when acting for the party in the superior position to avoid a challenge later on.

Part B

RECENT LEGISLATION

1   Access to the countryside

1.1 The Access to the Countryside (Means of Access, Appeals) (England) Regulations 2004

SI 2004/3305

Commencement date: 6 January 2005

These Regulations provide for the period within which, and the manner in which, appeals under section 38(1) of the Countryside and Rights of Way Act 2000 are to be brought and also make provision for the advertising of these appeals and for the appeal procedures. In particular:

- Part 2 (Regulations 4-12) of these Regulations relate to the initial stages of an appeal and include provision that:

  i) appeals are to be made by notice on a form obtained from the Secretary of State (Regulation 4(1));

  ii) an appeal against a notice under section 36(3) of the Act shall be made within the period specified in that notice within which the works specified in that notice are to be carried out (Regulation 4(2)(a)); and

  iii) an appeal against a notice under section 37(1) of the Act shall be made within the period specified in that notice after which the access authority intend to carry out the works specified in that notice (Regulation 4(2)(b));

- Part 3, Chapters I to III (Regulations 13-36) of these Regulations relate to the determination of these appeals and set out the procedures for:

i) appeals to be determined on the basis of written representations (Chapter I, Regulations 13-15);

ii) appeals to be determined by way of a hearing (Chapter II, Regulations 16-24); and

iii) appeals to be determined by way of an inquiry (Chapter III, Regulations 25-36).

- Part 3, Chapter IV (Regulations 37-42) of these Regulations contains general provisions, including provision for allowing further time for taking any step required by these Regulations (Regulation 38) and provision for the inspection and copying of documents (Regulation 39).

| 2 | **Commonhold and leasehold reform** |

2.1 The Commonhold and Leasehold Reform Act 2002 (Commencement No 4) Order 2004

SI 2004/1832

Commencement date: 27 September 2004

This Order brought into force, on 27 September 2004, Part 1 of the Commonhold and Leasehold Reform Act 2002, save for section 21(4) and (5), so far as it is not already in force.

2.2 The Commonhold and Leasehold Reform Act 2002 (Commencement No 5 and Saving and Transitional Provision) Order 2004

SI 2004/3056

Commencement date: 17 November 2004 and 28 February 2005

This Order brought into force further provisions of Part 2 (leasehold reform) of the Commonhold and Leasehold Reform Act 2002.

Article 2 brought into force, in England and Wales, on the day after this Order was made, the repeal of section 104 of the 2002 Act. That section amended the Land Registration Act 1925, to allow for notice to be entered in the register in respect of the right to manage. Following the repeal of the 1925 Act, section 104 is now redundant.

The provisions in article 3 came into force, in relation to England only, on 28th February 2005. They include:

a) provisions amending section 18(1) of, and Schedule 6 to, the Leasehold Reform, Housing and Urban Development Act 1993. The principal effect of the amendments is that the price to be paid for the freehold, where it is bought by qualifying tenants, will reflect the value of the interests held by all the landlords in the property concerned, at the date on which notice of the claim to exercise the right to collective enfranchisement is given under section 13 of the 1993 Act. There is a relevant transitional provision in Article 4(1);

b) new provisions under which, in certain circumstances, long leaseholders may insure their houses otherwise than with an insurer nominated or approved by the landlord (section 164);

c) new provisions requiring landlords to notify long leaseholders that rent is due (section 166);

d) new provisions preventing the landlord of a long leaseholder from exercising a right of re-entry or forfeiture on account of the leaseholder's failure to pay rent, service or administration charges, where the unpaid amount and the period for which any part of it has been payable do not exceed the amount and period prescribed by Regulations (section 167);

e) new provisions preventing the landlord of a long leaseholder from serving a forfeiture notice in respect of a breach of covenant or condition in the lease unless the leaseholder admits the breach, or a court or arbitral tribunal has finally determined that the breach has occurred (sections 168 and 169). There is a saving, relevant to section 168, in Article 4(2); and

f) changes to the conditions that must be satisfied before the landlord of a long leaseholder can exercise a right of re-entry or forfeiture for failure to pay service charges (section 170). There is a relevant saving in Article 4(3).

2.3 The Commonhold and Leasehold Reform Act 2002 (Commencement No 5 and Saving and Transitional Provision) (Amendment) (England) Order 2005

SI 2005/193

Commencement date: 28 February 2005

This Order amends Article 4 of the Commonhold and Leasehold Reform Act 2002 (Commencement No. 5 and Saving and Transitional Provision) Order 2004, which brought into force on 28 February 2005, in relation to England, provisions of Part 2 (leasehold reform) of the Commonhold and Leasehold Reform Act 2002 relating to the collective enfranchisement by tenants of flats.

The new saving provision inserted by this Order means that the changes made by section 126 of the 2002 Act will not have effect where notice is given under section 13 of the Leasehold Reform, Housing and Urban Development Act 1993, or application for a vesting order is made under section 26 of the 1993 Act, before 28 February 2005.

3   Competition law

3.1   The Competition Act 1998 (Land Agreements Exclusion and Revocation) Order 2004

SI 2004/1260

Commencement date: 1 May 2005

This Order excludes land agreements from the prohibition on anti-competitive agreements imposed by section 2 of the Competition Act 1998. The Order provides for a power to withdraw the exclusion from a particular agreement, and that an agreement to the like object or effect between the same parties to an agreement, from which the exclusion is withdrawn, is not excluded.

4   Compulsory purchase

4.1   The Compulsory Purchase of Land (Written Representations Procedure) (National Assembly for Wales) Regulations 2004

SI 2004/2730

Commencement date: 31 October 2004

These Regulations set out the written representations procedure that may be used for deciding whether to authorise the compulsory purchase of land in Wales, where the National Assembly for Wales is the acquiring or confirming authority and the procedures in the Acquisition of Land Act 1981 apply.

Objections to the confirmation of a compulsory purchase order made under Part II of the Act (as defined in section 13A(1) of the Act) which have not been withdrawn and which may not be disregarded ('remaining objections') can be determined by a procedure prescribed by regulations (section 13A of the Act). This is an alternative to the holding of an inquiry, provided all those having remaining objections consent in the prescribed manner.

Similarly, remaining objections to the making of a compulsory purchase order under Schedule 1 to the Act (as defined in paragraph 4A(1) of Schedule 1 to the Act) can be determined by such a procedure (paragraph 4A of Schedule 1 to the Act).

The main steps in the procedure are as follows:

- If the National Assembly is considering the use of the procedure, it will send a consent form (in the form set out in the Schedule to these Regulations) to all those with remaining objections, seeking their written consent to the use of the procedure (Regulation 3).

- Only if all such objectors consent may the National Assembly use the procedure. It is not obliged to use the procedure but, if it determines that the procedure should apply, it will set a starting date from which the procedure will commence (Regulation 4).

- Any documents served by the acquiring authority on the remaining objectors at the time of the making or preparation in draft of a compulsory purchase order, and any letters and other documents provided to the National Assembly as objections to confirmation or making, will form part of the representations to be considered (Regulation 5(1) and (2)).

- Unless the acquiring authority elects not to do so, it may make representations in support of its application (which may be disregarded if received more than 14 working days after the starting date). Such representations will be copied to each remaining objector (Regulation 5(4) and (5));

- Any remaining objector may make representations in response (which may be disregarded if received more than 15 working days after the National Assembly sends a copy of the acquiring authority's representations under paragraph (d) above) (Regulation 5(6) and (7));

- In response to a remaining objector's representations mentioned in paragraph (e) above, the acquiring authority may make further representations (which may be disregarded if received more than 10 working days after the National Assembly or, if different, the acquiring authority sends a copy of the remaining objectors' representations) (Regulation 5(8) and (9)).

- The National Assembly may permit representations to be made by any other person (which may be disregarded if received more than 14 working days after the starting date set for the acquiring authority to provide its representations) (Regulation 6).

- The National Assembly has discretion to extend the time limits in any particular case (Regulation 7).

- The National Assembly may appoint an inspector to consider the representations, to undertake a site inspection (if appropriate) and to report in writing to the National Assembly with a recommendation (Regulation 8).

- The inspector may, at any time, make a site inspection of the land which is the subject of the compulsory purchase order and of the surrounding area. The inspector may make the inspection unaccompanied (without giving prior notice to the acquiring authority and the remaining objectors), or in the company of a representative of the acquiring authority and the remaining objectors (Regulation 9(1)). Notification of the date and time of an accompanied inspection must be sent to the acquiring authority, and the remaining objectors, by the National Assembly so as to be received not less than five working days before the inspection (Regulation 9(2)). The inspector is not required to defer an accompanied inspection where the acquiring authority or a remaining objector is not present (Regulation 9(3)).

- If, not later than 10 working days after the starting date, the acquiring authority or a remaining objector makes to the National Assembly a request for an accompanied site inspection, such an inspection must be arranged by the National Assembly (Regulation 9(4)).

- The National Assembly will determine the confirmation or making of the compulsory purchase order on the basis of the written representations and any report of the inspector (Regulation 10).

- The National Assembly will (unless it is the acquiring authority) notify the acquiring authority, and those permitted to make representations in respect of their objections, of the decision and the reasons for the decision. Any such person may apply for a copy of any report or representation taken into account; such report or representations, then to be sent not later than ten working days after receipt of the request (Regulation 11).

4.2 The Compulsory Purchase of Land (Prescribed Forms) (National Assembly for Wales) Regulations 2004

SI 2004/2732

Commencement date: 31 October 2004

These Regulations re-enact, with amendments, the Compulsory Purchase of Land Regulations 1994 (SI 1994/2145) by prescribing forms for use in connection with the compulsory purchase of land which is – and the compulsory purchase of new rights over land which are – subject to the procedures contained in the Acquisition of Land Act 1981 where the acquiring or confirming authority is the National Assembly for Wales.

The amendments take account of the legislative changes in the Planning and Compulsory Purchase Act 2004 and make further minor drafting changes.

The main features of those amendments are to provide:

a) prescribed forms for an extended category of person (referred as a 'qualifying person') who is to be served with notice of the making of a compulsory purchase order (section 12(1) of the 1981 Act). The prescribed forms are amended to provide for the inclusion of this extended category in the Schedule to a compulsory purchase order (Forms 1 to 6);

b) a prescribed form for a notice of the making or preparation in draft of a compulsory purchase order which is to be affixed to a conspicuous object or objects on or near the land comprised in the order (section 11(3) of, and paragraph 2(3) of Schedule 1 to, the 1981 Act) (Form 7). This is the same prescribed form as for the newspaper notice advertising the compulsory purchase order;

c) a prescribed form for a notice of the National Assembly's confirmation or making of a compulsory purchase order which is to be affixed to a conspicuous object or objects on or near the land comprised in the compulsory purchase order (section 15(1)(b) of, and paragraph 6(1)(b) of Schedule 1 to, the 1981 Act) (Form 10). This is the same prescribed form as for the newspaper notice advertising the confirmation or making of the compulsory purchase order; and

d) a prescribed form for a notice of confirmation when the acquiring authority confirms an unopposed compulsory purchase order following notification by the National Assembly in accordance with section 14A of the 1981 Act (Form 11).

The forms contained in the Schedule to these Regulations enable an acquiring authority to use the Welsh and/or English language as that authority considers appropriate.

4.3 The Compulsory Purchase of Land (Prescribed Forms) (Ministers) Regulations 2004

SI 2004/2595

Commencement date: 31 October 2004

These Regulations re-enact, with amendments, the Compulsory Purchase of Land Regulations 1994. They prescribe forms for use in connection with the compulsory purchase of land and new rights over land in England and Wales which are subject to the procedures contained in the Acquisition of Land Act 1981, except when the acquiring or confirming authority is the National Assembly for Wales. The amendments take account of the legislative changes in the Planning and Compulsory Purchase Act 2004 as well as minor changes in drafting.

4.4 The Compulsory Purchase of Land (Written Representations Procedure) (Ministers) Regulations 2004

SI 2004/2594

Commencement date: 31 October 2004

These Regulations set out the written representations procedure that may be used for deciding whether to authorise the compulsory purchase of land in England and Wales. They apply only when the acquiring or confirming authority is a Minister of the Crown. The procedure may only be used for compulsory purchase orders that are subject to the Acquisition of Land Act 1981 and not subject to special parliamentary procedure.

4.5 The Home Loss Payments (Prescribed Amounts) (England) Regulations 2004

SI 2004/1631

Commencement date: 1 September 2004

These Regulations increase the amount of home loss payments

payable under the Land Compensation Act 1973 prescribed in the Home Loss Payments (England) Regulations 2003. Regulation 2(1)(a) increases the amount payable, where a person occupying a dwelling on the date of displacement has an owner's interest, from £31,000 to £34,000 and Regulation 2(1)(b) increases the minimum amount from £3,100 to £3,400. Regulation 2(2) increases the home loss payment in any other case from £3,100 to £3,400. The revised amounts apply where the displacement occurs on or after 1 September 2004.

4.6 The Home Loss Payments (Prescribed Amounts) (Wales) Regulations 2004

SI 2004/1758 (W 189)

Commencement date: 1 September 2004

These Regulations, which apply to Wales, increase the maximum and minimum amounts of home loss payments payable under the Land Compensation Act 1973 ('the Act') to those with an owner's interest in a dwelling. They also increase the amount of home loss payment payable in any other case. Regulation 2(a) increases the amount payable, where a person occupying a dwelling on the date of displacement has an owner's interest, from £31,000 to £34,000 and Regulation 2(b) increases the minimum amount from £3,100 to £3,400. Regulation 2(c) increases the home loss payment in any other case from £3,100 to £3,400. The revised amounts apply where the displacement occurs on or after 1 September 2004.

5   Financial services

5.1 The Financial Services and Markets Act 2000 (Designated Professional Bodies) (Amendment) Order 2004

SI 2004/3352

Commencement date: 14 January 2005

This Order makes the Council for Licensed Conveyancers a designated professional body for the purposes of Part 20 of the Financial Services and Markets Act 2000. This enables members of the Council of Licensed Conveyancers (subject to certain conditions set out in section 327 of the Act) to be exempt from the requirement to obtain permission from the Financial Services Authority in order to carry out certain regulated activities.

6   High hedges

6.1   The Anti-social Behaviour Act 2003 (Commencement No 3) (Wales) Order 2004
SI 2004/3238 (W 281)

Commencement date: 31 December 2004

This Order brought into force, on 31 December 2004, the provisions of Part 8 of the Anti-social Behaviour Act 2003 in relation to hedges situated in Wales. Part 8 of the Act gives local authorities the power to deal with complaints about high hedges which are having an adverse effect on a neighbour's enjoyment of his or her property. It also gives the National Assembly for Wales the power to make regulations, in relation to hedges situated in Wales, to set the maximum level of fee chargeable by a local authority for dealing with an application under the Act and to set out the procedures to be followed where an appeal is made to the National Assembly under section 71 of the Act.

6.2   The High Hedges (Appeals) (Wales) Regulations 2004
SI 2004/3240 (W 282)

Commencement date: 31 December 2004

Section 71 of the Anti-social Behaviour Act 2003 sets out the various rights of appeal against a local authority's decisions under section 68 of the Act (procedure for dealing with complaints) and under section 70 of the Act (withdrawal, waiver or relaxation of remedial notices), and against any remedial notice issued by the local authority. In relation to hedges situated in Wales, an appeal must be made to the National Assembly. In its capacity as the appeal authority in relation to hedges situated in Wales, section 72 of the Act gives the National Assembly the power to make regulations to:

a) provide the procedure for dealing with appeals under Part 8 of the Act (including specifying the grounds on which appeals may be made);

b) appoint another person to hear and determine appeals; and

c) require an appointed person to carry out all or any of the National Assembly's functions in relation to such appeals.

The National Assembly may allow or dismiss an appeal, completely or in part. If the National Assembly allows an appeal, it may quash or vary the remedial notice to which the appeal relates and may also issue a remedial notice where the local authority decided not to do so when it dealt with the original complaint. Whatever its decision on an appeal, the National Assembly may correct any defect, error or misdescription in the original remedial notice if it considers no injustice will be caused in doing so.

6.3 The High Hedges (Fees) (Wales) Regulations 2004

SI 2004/3241 (W 283)

Commencement date: 31 December 2004

A complaint must be made to the local authority in whose area the land on which the hedge is situated lies, and must be accompanied by a fee determined by the local authority (subject to a maximum amount prescribed in regulations made, in relation to hedges situated in Wales, by the National Assembly for Wales). These Regulations prescribe that maximum amount.

7 Housing

7.1 The Housing Act 2004

The Housing Act 2004 received Royal Assent on 18 November 2004. This Act replaces the existing housing fitness standard with the Housing Health and Safety Rating System. It introduces two new licensing regimes for private rented properties. There is a new requirement for sellers or estate agents to produce a home information pack before marketing any residential property for sale along with provision for an ombudsman scheme for estate agents. The Act makes other provisions about housing, including changing the right to buy scheme, strengthening the rights of park home owners, extending the power of the Housing Corporation to give social housing grant to non-registered social landlords and enabling local authorities to secure occupation of long-term empty private sector homes. It also establishes tenancy deposit schemes to safeguard deposits paid in connection with assured shorthold tenancies. Finally, it requires local housing authorities to assess the accommodation needs of gypsies and travellers in their area, and produce a strategy on how these needs can be met.

The Act is divided into seven parts:

Part 1 – Housing conditions;

Part 2 – Licensing of houses in multiple occupation;

Part 3 – Selective licensing of other residential accommodation;

Part 4 – Additional control provisions in relation to residential accommodation;

Part 5 – Home information packs;

Part 6 – Other provisions about housing;

Part 7 – Supplementary and final provisions.

Part 1: Housing conditions

Part 1 of the Act replaces the existing housing fitness standard contained in the Housing Act 1985 with the Housing Health and Safety Rating System. It also adapts and extends the powers of enforcement currently available to local housing authorities to tackle poor housing conditions. These changes are intended to help local housing authorities to prioritise their intervention based on the severity of the health and safety hazards in the home.

Part 2: Licensing of houses in multiple occupation

Part 2 of the Act introduces a mandatory scheme to license houses in multiple occupation ('HMOs') of a description contained in regulations. It is intended initially to apply this only to the larger, higher risk HMOs of three or more storeys occupied by five or more people. Local housing authorities are given power to extend licensing in their districts to other categories of HMO, subject to carrying out consultation and with the approval of the appropriate national authority.

Part 3: Selective licensing of other residential accommodation

Part 3 of the Act provides a power for local housing authorities to introduce selective licensing to deal with particular problems in an area. Selective licensing will be primarily focused on areas of low housing demand, or that are likely to fall into that category, and other areas suffering from anti-social behaviour.

The Act provides a discretionary power, subject to carrying out consultation and to the approval of the appropriate national authority, for local housing authorities to license all private landlords in a designated area with the intention of ensuring that a minimum standard of management is met. In order for a scheme to be approved, such a selective licensing scheme must be shown to be co-ordinated with an authority's wider strategies to deal with anti-social behaviour and regeneration.

The Act also provides the appropriate national authority with powers to prescribe by regulation other circumstances in which discretionary schemes may be made.

Part 4: Additional control provisions in relation to residential accommodation

Chapter 1 of Part 4 contains provisions for enforcement action in respect of properties licensable under Parts 2 and 3 and for individual properties where a residential property tribunal is satisfied that a property, which is not required to be licensed, requires the intervention of the local housing authority. Chapter 2 enables local housing authorities to take over the management of long-term empty properties and to bring them back into occupation. Chapter 3 contains provisions on overcrowding in non-licensable HMOs.

Part 5: Home information packs

Part 5 of the Act imposes new legal duties on people marketing residential properties in England and Wales. Before marketing a property, the seller (or, more usually, their estate agent) must have a home information pack of standard documents available for prospective buyers.

Part 6: Other provisions about housing

The Act gives local housing authorities further tools to tackle anti-social behaviour in social housing. These measures complement those introduced by the Anti-social Behaviour Act 2003.

Part 6 introduces changes to the Right to Buy scheme. This is a statutory scheme enabling secure tenants to buy the homes that they live in, at a discount, from their landlord. Landlords are most often local housing authorities, but registered social landlords (and certain other social landlords) may also have tenants who have the Right to Buy, or preserved Right to Buy, both for historical reasons and as a result of large-scale voluntary transfers of properties from local housing authority ownership. Provisions in the Act will amend the Right to Buy scheme with a view to tackling exploitation of the rules by property developers and tenants.

Part 6 also contains provisions to better protect park home owners. These changes will help deter unscrupulous site owners from exploiting and harassing occupiers, and give a power to the Secretary of State to make further changes to the implied terms of occupation agreements.

Changes have been made to bring the treatment of local authority owned gypsy and traveller sites into line with that for privately owned caravan sites, with regard to protection from unlawful eviction and harassment.

The powers of the Housing Corporation and the National Assembly for Wales under the Housing Act 1996 are extended to allow them to give grants to persons other than registered social landlords for specified purposes.

Part 6 extends eligibility for disabled facilities grant to include all those occupying caravans as their only or main residence.

A duty has been introduced upon local housing authorities to carry out assessments of the accommodation needs of gypsies and travellers residing in or resorting to their district, when they undertake a review of housing needs in the district.

Part 6 sets up the office of Social Housing Ombudsman for Wales to investigate complaints against social landlords in Wales.

Part 6 also establishes tenancy deposit schemes. These will protect tenants' deposits in the private rented sector and help to ensure that such deposits are not misappropriated by landlords or their agents.

Part 7: Supplementary and final provisions

Part 7 requires local housing authorities to keep registers of licences and management orders. It also provides for the approval of statutory codes of management practice, and for the making of management regulations, relating to HMOs.

For the purposes of Parts 1 to 4 of the Act, it provides for documents and other information to be produced. It provides powers of entry to property and powers to prescribe the form of any notice, statement or other document required or authorised under the Act.

7.2 The Housing Benefit (General) (Amendment) Regulations 2004

SI 2004/2984

Commencement date: 9 December 2004

These Regulations further amended the Housing Benefit (General) Regulations 1987, which provide for a scheme whereby housing benefit is payable to persons who are liable to make certain payments in respect of a dwelling occupied as their home.

7.3 The Rent Officers (Housing Benefit Functions) (Student Accommodation) Amendment Order 2004

SI 2004/2101

Commencement date: 31 August 2004

This Order amended the definition of 'assured tenancy' in the Rent Officers (Housing Benefit Functions) Order 1997 which confers on rent officers functions in relation to the determination of eligible rent for the purposes of claims for housing benefit under Part VII of the Social Security Contributions and Benefits Act 1992 Orders to include, within that definition, tenancies granted to students (in particular by educational institutions), so that a rent officer may take account of rent levels in student accommodation when making determinations for the purposes of that Order.

7.4 The Demoted Tenancies (Review of Decisions) (England) Regulations 2004

SI 2004/1679

Commencement date: 30 July 2004

Section 14 of the Anti-social Behaviour Act 2003 amended Part 4 of the Housing Act 1985 to allow a secure tenancy of a local housing authority, a housing action trust or a registered social landlord to be brought to an end and replaced with a less secure demoted tenancy by a demotion order made by a county court. Schedule 1 to the 2003 Act inserted further provisions regarding demoted tenancies as a new Chapter 1A of Part 5 of the Housing Act 1996. If a landlord wishes to end a demoted tenancy, it must serve the tenant with a notice stating that the landlord has decided to apply to the court for an order for possession, setting out the reasons for that decision and informing the tenant of his right to request a review of the decision. These Regulations make provision about the procedure to be followed in such a review.

Regulation 2 provides that a review must be undertaken by a person who was not involved in the original decision. If the original decision was made by an officer, then any review of that decision by another officer may only be carried out by an officer occupying a more senior position within the landlord's organisation than the officer who made the original decision.

Regulation 3 requires the landlord to give the tenant notice of the date of the review.

Regulation 4 enables the tenant to obtain an oral hearing in certain circumstances and explains how that right may be exercised.

Regulations 5 to 9 set out the details of the review procedure.

7.5 The Secure Tenancies (Notices) (Amendment) (England) Regulations 2004

SI 2004/1627

Commencement date: 19 July 2004

These Regulations amended the Secure Tenancies (Notices) Regulations 1987, as they apply in England, to prescribe the form of notice which should be served on a secure tenant before a landlord begins proceedings for a demotion order under section 82A.

7.6 The Housing Act 2004 (Commencement No 1) (England) Order 2005

SI 2005/326

Commencement date: 17 February 2005

This Order brought the following provisions of the Housing Act 2004 into force in England on 17 February 2005:

- Section 220 (which extends the powers of the Housing Corporation to give grants to persons other than registered social landlords).

- Section 221 (which is related to section 220 and which extends the right to acquire, in relation to a dwelling provided by means of a grant, to a person other than a registered social landlord);

- Section 227 (which removes the duty on local housing authorities to send annual reports to tenants).

8 Land registration

8.1 The Land Registration Fee Order 2004

SI 2004/595

Commencement date: 1 April 2004

This Order replaced the Land Registration Fee Order 2003 and makes the following changes to land registration fees:

- Scale 1 (which sets out the fees for applications for first registration of title to land and to transfers of, and certain leases out of, registered land for monetary consideration) is amended by the reduction of the fee for applications within the three highest bands; £200,001-£500,000, £500,001-£1,000,000 and £1,000,001 and over.

- Unlike previous orders, this Order contains no provision for the registrar to retain any overpayment in respect of the cost of its repayment.

- Also, unlike previous orders, this Order does not include a provision enabling the registrar to waive a fee in whole or part, or any category of fee, which is contained in either Article 4(1)(g) or Schedule 3. As a result, certain applications formerly treated under the waiver have been added to the category of exemptions (Schedule 4).

- In particular, because there is no waiver provision, the Order provides that an official search of the index map attracts no fee if the search result discloses no more than ten registered titles; but there is a fee of £4 for each additional title if the result discloses more than ten titles (Schedule 3, Part 3(5) and Schedule 4(15)).

- There is no longer a provision for the registrar to charge an additional fee, to cover the excess cost of the work involved, in respect of applications for a search of the index map, or for the determination of the exact line of a boundary.

- The separate categorisation for fee purposes of applications comprising land having an area or aggregate area exceeding 100 hectares, which were known as 'large area applications', has been discontinued; such applications will now fall to be assessed under Scale 1 or Article 6.

- The Order also changed the basis of fee assessment for an application for which no other fee is payable under the Order, from one related to value and the work involved to a fixed fee of £40 (Article 12).

8.2 The Land Registration Fee (Amendment) Order 2004
SI 2004/1833

Commencement date: In accordance with Article 1(1)

This Order amended the Land Registration Fee Order 2004 so as to prescribe fees for applications made under the Commonhold and Leasehold Reform Act 2002. It provides that, where such an application relates to the freehold estate in commonhold land registered in the name of the developer, the fee will be unaffected by the number of such titles.

8.3 The Commonhold (Land Registration) Rules 2004
SI 2004/1830

Commencement date: In accordance with rule 1

These rules provide, for applications to the Registrar under the Commonhold and Leasehold Reform Act 2002, the form of the documentation which must accompany any application and the circumstances in which an application may be cancelled by the Registrar. Schedule 1 contains the prescribed forms and Schedule 2 prescribes the wording of the restrictions prescribed by the rules.

9 Landlord and tenant

9.1 The Service Charges (Consultation Requirements) (Amendment) (No 2) (England) Regulations 2004
SI 2004/2939

Commencement date: 12 November 2004

These Regulations correct errors in SI 2004/2665 and revoke it. They amend Regulation 4 of the Service Charges (Consultation Requirements) (England) Regulations 2003, which provides for the application of section 20 of the Landlord and Tenant Act 1985 to certain agreements entered into, by or on behalf of a landlord or superior landlord, for a term of more than twelve months ('qualifying long term agreements'), where relevant costs (defined in section 18(2) of the 1985 Act) incurred under the agreement in any accounting period exceed an amount which results in the relevant contribution of any tenant, in respect of that period, being more than £100. Section 20 of the 1985 Act imposes limitations on the amount of tenants' contributions to service charges in respect of qualifying long-term agreements, unless the consultation requirements in the Service Charges (Consultation Requirements) (England) Regulations 2003 have been complied with or dispensed with by a leasehold valuation tribunal.

The amendments made by the Regulations affect any landlord who intends to enter into a qualifying long-term agreement on or after 12 November 2004, but only if he or she has not previously made up service charge accounts referable to a qualifying long-term agreement in respect of the dwellings to which the intended agreement is to relate.

The Regulations modify the operation of paragraph (3) of Regulation 4, which relates to the definition of the term 'accounting period' that is used in paragraph (1) of that Regulation. Section 20 of the 1985 Act will apply in the circumstances mentioned above if the relevant contribution of any tenant to relevant costs to be incurred under the agreement in the period of twelve months, beginning with the relevant date, exceed £100. For this purpose, the relevant date is the date marking the beginning of the first period for which service charges are payable by a tenant under a lease of a dwelling to which the intended agreement relates. The effect of paragraphs (2) and (4) of Regulation 4 is that each subsequent accounting period will be a period of twelve months beginning as soon as the previous accounting period has ended.

9.2 The Approval of Codes of Management Practice (Residential Property) (England) Order 2004

SI 2004/1802

Commencement date: 10 August 2004

By this Order, the First Secretary of State approved a code of practice relating to the management of residential property by landlords and others who discharge the management function. The approved code is the *Rent Only Residential Management Code* (ISBN 184219 070 9) and is published by the Royal Institution of Chartered Surveyors. The First Secretary of State also withdraws the approval given in the Approval of Codes of Management Practice (Residential Property) Order 1996 (SI 1996/2839) for the previous code, also called the *Rent Only Residential Management Code* (ISBN 085406 642 X).

Section 87(7) of the Leasehold Reform, Housing and Urban Development Act 1996 provides that failure to comply with any provision of an approved code of practice does not of itself render any person liable to any proceedings but, in any proceedings, the code of practice shall be admissible as evidence, and any provision which appears to be relevant to any question arising in the proceedings shall be taken into account.

9.3 The Landlord and Tenant Act 1954, Part 2 (Notices) Regulations 2004

SI 2004/1005

Commencement date: 1 June 2004

These Regulations replaced the Landlord and Tenant Act 1954, Part II (Notices) Regulations 1983. Regulation 3 prescribes the form of various notices relevant to business tenancies. The prescribed forms are set out in Schedule 2. Forms that are substantially to the same effect as those prescribed may be used (Regulation 2(2)). The purposes for which the prescribed forms are to be used are specified in Schedule 1. The forms reflect amendments to Part 2 of the Landlord and Tenant Act 1954 made by the Regulatory Reform (Business Tenancies) (England and Wales) Order 2003 (SI 2003/3096). Regulation 4 revokes the Landlord and Tenant Act 1954, Part II (Notices) Regulations 1983 and the Landlord and Tenant Act 1954, Part II (Notices) (Amendment) Regulations 1989.

9.4 The Rights of Re-entry and Forfeiture (Prescribed Sum and Period) (England) Regulations 2004

SI 2004/3086

Commencement date: 23 November 2004

Section 167(1) of the Commonhold and Leasehold Reform Act 2002 prevents a landlord under a long lease of a dwelling from exercising a right of re-entry or forfeiture for failure by a tenant to pay an amount consisting of rent, service charges or administration charges (or a combination of them), unless the unpaid amount exceeds the prescribed sum or consists of, or includes, an amount which has been payable for more than a prescribed period. Regulation 2 prescribes the sum of £350 and a period of three years.

9.5 The Landlord and Tenant (Notice of Rent) (England) Regulations 2004

SI 2004/3096

Commencement date: 28 February 2005

These Regulations relate to the form and content of notices requiring the payment of ground rent. Regulation 2 supplements section 166(2) of the Commonhold and Leasehold Reform Act 2002, which requires a notice under section 166(1), relating to the payment of ground rent, to specify the amount due, the date on which the tenant is liable to make the payment and, if different, the date on which the tenant would have been liable to make the payment in accordance with the lease. The additional requirements specified in Regulation 2 include the provision of notes for both leaseholders and landlords. The content of the notes is set out in the Schedule to the Regulations, as part of the prescribed form of notice under section 166(1).

9.6 The Leasehold Houses (Notice of Insurance Cover) (England) Regulations 2004

SI 2004/3097

Commencement date: 28 February 2005

Where a long lease of a house requires the tenant to insure it with an insurer nominated or approved by the landlord, a tenant may avoid that requirement if the provisions of section 164(2)(a) to (d) relating to the insurer (the interests and risks covered and the amount of the cover) are satisfied and he gives a notice of cover to the landlord within the period specified in that section. A notice of cover must specify the name of the insurer, the risks covered by the policy, the amount and period of the cover and such further information as may be prescribed.

These Regulations prescribe the further information that is to be included in a notice of cover. That information is:

a) the address of the house insured under the policy;

b) the registered office of the insurer or, if the insurer does not have a registered office, its head office;

c) the number of the policy;

d) the frequency with which premiums are payable under the policy;

e) the amount of any excess payable by the tenant under the policy;

f) where an excess is payable, whether it is payable in respect of every claim made under the policy or only in particular circumstances and, if the latter, a brief description of those circumstances;

g) whether the policy has been renewed and, if so, the date on which it was last renewed;

h) if the policy has not been renewed, the date on which it took effect;

i) a statement that the tenant is satisfied that the policy covers his or her interests; and

j) a statement that the tenant has no reason to believe that the policy does not cover the interests of the landlord.

The notice may be in the form set out in the Schedule to the Regulations or in a form substantially to the same effect.

9.7 The Leasehold Valuation Tribunals (Procedure) (Amendment) (England) Regulations 2004

SI 2004/3098

Commencement date: 28 February 2005

These Regulations amend the Leasehold Valuation Tribunals (Procedure) (England) Regulations 2003 ('the Procedure Regulations').

The amendments made by Regulations 3, 4(b), 7 and 8(c) are consequential on the commencement of section 168 of the Commonhold and Leasehold Reform Act 2002. Section 168 prevents a landlord from serving a notice to forfeit a lease for breach by a tenant of a covenant or condition in the lease, unless the tenant admits the breach or it has been finally determined that the breach has occurred. Under subsection (4) of that section, a landlord may apply to a leasehold valuation tribunal for a determination that a breach of covenant or condition has occurred. The effect of the amendments made by Regulations 3, 4(b), 7 and 8 is to add applications under section 168(4) to the applications to which the Procedure Regulations apply, and to require the applicant to include with his application a statement giving particulars of the alleged breach of covenant or condition, and a copy of the lease concerned.

The amendment made by Regulation 4(a) has effect as regards applications, to a leasehold valuation tribunal under section 20ZA(1) of the Landlord and Tenant 1985 Act, to dispense with all or any of the consultation requirements relating to works and agreements for which contributions may be recovered by way of service charges. The effect of the amendment is to remove the requirement (imposed by Regulation 3(3) of, and paragraph 2(3) of Schedule 2 to, the Procedure Regulations) to provide a copy of the lease when making an application under section 20ZA(1).

The amendment made by Regulation 5 enables a leasehold valuation tribunal to determine an application without an oral hearing where it has given at least 28 days' notice to the applicant and the respondent and neither of them has asked for an oral hearing. (Regulation 13(3), which enables the tribunal to decide at any time before an application has been determined that it should be the subject of an oral hearing, and allows either of the parties to request an oral hearing at any time before the application has been determined, is unaffected by this amendment.)

The amendment made by Regulation 6 removes from Regulation 17 of the Procedure Regulations the requirement to give notice at the hearing where an inspection is to be made during or after the close of the hearing. The requirement to give at least 14 days' notice to the parties of the date, time and place of the inspection remains unchanged, but the opportunity has been taken to make minor drafting changes.

The amendments made by Regulation 8(a) and (b) require the production of a copy of the lease with certain applications relating to enfranchisement or lease extension, and with applications under Part 4 of the 1987 Act for the variation of a lease.

9.8 The Leasehold Houses (Notice of Insurance Cover) (England) (Amendment) Regulations 2005

SI 2005/177

Commencement date: 28 February 2005

These Regulations amend the Leasehold Houses (Notice of Insurance Cover) (England) Regulations 2004 by substituting paragraph 10 of the Schedule to those Regulations. That Schedule sets out the prescribed form of notice of cover, and paragraph 10 contains wording relevant to the requirement in Regulation 3(j) of the Regulations that the notice of cover must specify that the tenant has no reason to believe that the policy does not cover the interests of the landlord.

The amendment made by these Regulations has the effect of removing square brackets, which had been inserted in paragraph 10 in error and which gave the misleading impression that the paragraph could be omitted from a notice of cover.

10   Licensing

10.1 The Licensing Act 2003 (Transitional Provisions) Order 2005

SI 2005/40

Commencement date: 7 February 2005

This Order makes provision for the detailed requirements to be fulfilled by applicants to convert existing authorisations to use premises for the sale and supply of alcohol, the provision of regulated entertainment and the provision of late night refreshment to new premises licences under Schedule 8 to the Licensing Act 2003. It also makes provision for the detailed requirements to be fulfilled by a registered club under the Licensing Act 1964 to convert authorisations under its existing registration certificate to a new club premises certificate under Schedule 8 to the Act. In both cases, the Order prescribes the application form to be used by the applicant or club, the information to be supplied and the plan to accompany the application. Further, it prescribes the form to be used in relation to a simultaneous application to vary any existing authorisations (Articles 2, 3, 7 and 8). The Order requires the relevant licensing authority to provide application forms, etc., for applicants and clubs on request and provides a discretion to provide these on its website (Article 11).

Further, for the purposes of paragraphs 6(8) and 18(5) of Schedule 8 to the Act, this Order specifies the Children and Young Persons Act 1933, the Cinematograph (Safety) Regulations 1955 (SI 1955/1129), the Licensing Act 1964 and the Sporting Events (Control of Alcohol Etc) Act 1985 as enactments containing restrictions affecting existing authorisations which must be imposed as conditions on the new premises licence and the new club premises certificate (Articles 4 and 9).

Further, for the purposes of paragraph 11 of Schedule 8 to the Act in respect of opening hours of premises, the Order specifies the period commencing on 7 February 2005 and ending on the second appointed day as the period during which a relevant licensing authority may not grant a premises licence, subject to conditions which prevent the sale of alcohol on the premises during the permitted hours (subject to a minor disapplication); such hours being the hours during which the holder of a justices' licence is permitted to sell alcohol on the premises under Part 3 of the 1964 Act (Article 5). In addition, for the purposes of paragraph 12 of Schedule 8 to the Act in respect of a provisional grant of a justices' licence under the 1964 Act, this Order specifies the period commencing on 7 February 2005 and ending on the first anniversary of the second appointed day as the period during which the relevant licensing authority must have regard to that provisional grant when determining an application for the grant of a premises licence under Part 3 of the Act (Article 6).

Finally, for the purposes of an application for a personal licence under Part 6 of the Act made by the holder of a justices' licence, and for the purposes of paragraph 23 of Schedule 8 to the Act, the Order details the requirements in respect of a photograph to accompany the application (Article 10).

10.2 The Licensing Act 2003 (Personal Licences) Regulations 2005

SI 2005/41

Commencement date: 7 February 2005

These Regulations make provision for the detailed requirements to be fulfilled by applicants for personal licences under Part 6 of the Licensing Act 2003.

In addition, the Regulations prescribe those persons who do not possess a licensing qualification but to whom a licence may be granted (Regulation 4). The form of the personal licence is prescribed in Regulation 5.

The Regulations prescribe the application form to be used by the applicant, the information to be supplied and the documents to accompany the application for the grant or renewal of a personal licence (Regulations 6 and 7 and Schedules 1 to 3). In respect of an application for a personal licence made by the holder of a justices' licence during the period commencing on 7 February 2005 and ending on 6 August 2005, Regulation 8 and Schedules 3 and 4 prescribe the application form to be used by the applicant, the information to be supplied and the documents to accompany the application. In the case of such applications, reference should also be made to the Licensing Act 2003 (Transitional Provisions) Order 2005 (SI 2005/40).

The Regulations require the relevant licensing authority to provide the application forms for applicants on request and provides a discretion to provide these on its website.

10.3 The Licensing Act 2003 (Premises Licences and Club Premises Certificates) Regulations 2005

SI 2005/42

Commencement date: 7 February 2005

The Licensing Act 2003 provides for the licensing of premises for the sale by retail of alcohol, the supply of alcohol by or on behalf of a club to, or to the order of, a member of the club, the provision of regulated entertainment and the provision of late night refreshment. These Regulations set out the detailed requirements relating to applications, notices and representations given or made under Parts 3 and 4 of the Act and reviews made under those Parts and Part 8 of the Act.

In particular, these Regulations provide that weights and measures authorities are responsible authorities (Regulation 7). They also provide that persons with a prescribed interest in a premises include those with a legal interest as freeholder or leaseholder (Regulation 8) and Schedule 1 sets out the form of the notice to be given by a person to notify a relevant licensing authority of his, her or its interest in a licensed premises (Regulation 9).

Regulations 10 to 16 and Schedules 2 to 8 set out the form of applications and notices for the grant of a premises licence, the issue of a provisional statement, an application for variation of a premises licence, an application to vary a premises licence to specify the premises supervisor, an application to transfer a premises licence, the giving of an interim authority notice and an application for the review of a premises licence.

Regulations 17 to 20 and Schedules 9 and 10 set out the form of applications and declarations to be given by qualifying clubs. These include the form of the club declaration in which a club shows that it is a qualifying club, an application for a club premises certificate, and an application to vary a club premises certificate. Schedule 8 also sets out the form for an application to review a club premises certificate.

The Regulations provide that applications, notices and representations must be given or made in writing but includes a discretion for this requirement to be fulfilled by electronic means (Regulation 21).

Regulation 22 sets out the time limits during which representations must be made. Regulation 23 sets out the detailed requirements for plans of premises and club premises to be submitted with applications.

Regulation 24 and Schedule 11 set out the form of consents to be given by the premises supervisor of a premises and the holder of the premises licence in certain circumstances.

Regulations 25, 26, 38 and 39 set out the requirements for the advertisement of applications and reviews by applicants and by relevant licensing authorities.

Regulation 27 requires that persons or clubs applying for a premises licence, club premises certificate, provisional statement, variation of a premises licence or club premises certificate, review of a premises licence or club premises certificate, give notice of the application, by giving each responsible authority a copy of the application together with its accompanying documents on the same day as the day on which that application is given to the relevant licensing authority.

Further, Regulations 28 and 29 set out the requirements for giving of notices to the chief officer of police, the premises supervisor, the responsible authorities, the holder of the premises licence and the club holding the club premises certificate, in a number of circumstances where this is required by the Act.

Regulations 33 to 36 provide for the form of a premises licence and club premises certificate, and Regulation 30 states that they may not be granted to have effect until the second appointed day.

Regulations 31 and 32 provide that the notification from a licensing authority that any representation or a ground for review is frivolous, vexatious or repetitious, must be given in writing and as soon as reasonably practicable.

Regulation 37 sets out the requirements for the notice given by the relevant licensing authority to the holder of the premises licence and responsible authorities in respect of the review of a premises licence, following a closure order under Part 8 of the Act.

Regulations 40 and 41 provide that the relevant licensing authority must provide the forms listed in the Schedules to these Regulations on request, and that a licensing authority cannot reject any application or notice by reason only that it is given on a form provided from another source other than that relevant licensing authority. Finally, Regulation 42 requires the relevant licensing authority to acknowledge a notice received by it under section 178 of the Act.

10.4 The Licensing Act 2003 (Licensing Authority's Register) (Other Information) Regulations 2005

SI 2005/43

Commencement date: 7 February 2005

These Regulations prescribe the further information each licensing authority is required to record in the register it is required to keep under section 8 of the Licensing Act 2003. In addition to the records identified in section 8(1) of and Schedule 3 to the Act, each licensing authority must record in its register operating schedules and club operating schedules (or revisions of these) and plans of premises which accompany applications for premises licences or club premises certificates (or variations of these) and Schedules of works and plans of the work being or about to be done which accompany applications, for provisional statements (Regulation 2(2)). Further, each licensing authority must record in its register the ground or grounds for reviews set out in applications for a review of a premises licence or club premises certificate, and the determination of the magistrates' court on its consideration of a closure order (Regulation 2(3)). Finally, a record must be kept of the existing licensable activities and existing qualifying club activities and plans of the premises which accompany applications (for conversion of existing licences and existing club certificates (Regulation 2(4)).

10.5 The Licensing Act 2003 (Hearings) Regulations 2005

SI 2005/44

Commencement date: 7 February 2005

These Regulations make provision for the holding of hearings required to be held by licensing authorities under the Licensing Act 2003.

In particular, the Regulations provide for the timing of hearings and the notification requirements to parties to a hearing of the date, time and place of a hearing and information to accompany that notification (Regulations 4 to 7 and Schedules 1, 2 and 3). In addition, provision is made for a party to a hearing to provide information to the licensing authority about attendance at a hearing, representations, the seeking of permission for another person to attend to assist the authority and whether the party believes a hearing to be necessary (Regulation 8).

The Regulations provide for a range of procedural issues to govern the way in which preparations are made for a hearing, for the procedures to be followed, the rights of parties at a hearing, as well as various administrative matters, for example the keeping of a record of the hearing and the manner of giving notices (Regulations 9 to 33). The Regulations also make provision for the timing of the licensing authority's determination following a hearing (Schedule 4).

In so far as these Regulations do not make provision for procedures for and at hearings, section 9 of the Act provides that the authority can determine its own procedure.

10.6 The Licensing Act 2003 (Fees) Regulations 2005

SI 2005/79

Commencement date: 7 February 2005

These Regulations provide for the determination of the fees to accompany the making of applications and the giving of notices under the Licensing Act 2003 and the payment of those fees. Further, they make provision for the payment of annual fees in respect of premises licences and club premises certificates granted under the Act.

In particular, they provide for the manner in which premises are allocated to specific bands for the purposes of determining the appropriate level of fee to be paid when applying for a premises licence or club premises certificate, and for variations of the licences and certificates by reference mainly to the non-domestic value of the premises (Regulation 3 and Schedule 1).

The Regulations make provision for the fee levels in respect of applications for premises licences and also identify circumstances in which a particular application in respect of premises in the higher bands attracts a multiplier in respect of the fee, and when an additional fee needs to be paid in respect of events where 5,000 or more people may attend the premises concerned (Regulation 4 and Schedules 2 and 3). However, the Regulations disapply the requirement to pay the additional fee in respect of premises that are buildings when certain conditions are met (Regulation 4(5)). In respect of an application to vary which is made at the same time as an application to convert existing licences to new premises licences under paragraph 2 of Schedule 8 to the Act, the Regulations provide for a reduced fee to be paid for the application to vary (Regulation 4(6) and Schedule 4).

Provision is made for the payment of an annual fee and the timing of that payment in respect of premises licences, and provides for multipliers to be applied to the fee in relation to premises in higher bands and for the payment of an additional fee where the premises accommodate 5,000 or more people at the same time (Regulation 5 and Schedule 5). The requirement to pay an additional annual fee is disapplied in relation to premises that comprise a building, if certain conditions are met (Regulation 5(5)).

Similar provision is made in respect of applications for club premises certificates and variations of these, except that such applications do not attract multiplier fees or additional fees (Regulation 6 and Schedule 2). Also, provision is made for the payment of an annual fee in respect of club premises certificates and the timing of that payment. A duty is placed on the secretary of a club to pay the fee on behalf of the club (Regulation 7 and Schedule 5).

A number of fixed fees in relation to other applications made or notices given under the Act are provided for, for example in respect of the giving of a temporary event notice under Part 5 of the Act (Regulation 8 and Schedule 6).

Exemption from the payment of an application fee is provided in respect of applications relating only to regulated entertainment made in respect of certain premises where conditions are met – these being schools and colleges where the school or college premises are used for the entertainment by the school or college on behalf of the school or college or the use of church halls, village halls and the like for the provision of entertainment (Regulation 9). A similar exemption is provided from the requirement to pay an annual fee in these circumstances provided conditions are met at the time an annual fee falls due to be paid (Regulation 10).

Fees to be paid in respect of applications under paragraphs 2 or 14 of Schedule 8 to the Act are provided in the Licensing Act 2003 (Transitional Conversions Fees) Order 2005 (SI 2005/80).

10.7 The Licensing Act 2003 (Transitional Conversions Fees) Order 2005

SI 2005/80

Commencement date: 7 February 2005

This Order makes provision for the determination of the fees to be paid in respect of premises for the conversion of existing licences and registered certificates to new premises licences and club premises certificates under paragraphs 2 or 14 of Schedule 8 to the Licensing Act 2003.

Article 3 and Schedule 1 allocate premises to bands by reference to the non-domestic rateable value of premises and make provision about the relevant band in circumstances where the premises does not have a non-domestic rateable value and in other circumstances.

Articles 4 and 5 and Schedule 2 make provision for the level of fee to be paid, by reference to the band in which the premises is allocated and, for conversions to premises licences only, for a multiplier to be applied to the fee for higher banded premises. Article 4(4) and Schedule 3 make provision for an additional fee to be paid in respect of a conversion to a premises licence, where the number of persons the applicant allows on the premises at any one time is 5,000 or more. (Article 4(5) sets out circumstances in which this additional fee is not payable in respect of premises which comprise a building.)

Article 6 makes provision for exemption from paying the fee in respect of applications to convert which relate to the provision of regulated entertainment only in specified circumstances. These relate to schools and colleges (defined in Article 2) and to church halls, village halls and the like.

This Order does not make provision for any other fees payable in respect of applications made or notices given under the Act. In particular, it does not make provision for the fee in respect of applications to vary under sections 34, 37 or 84 of the Act made at the same time as the applications to convert covered by this Order. All other such fees are provided for in the Licensing Act 2003 (Fees) Regulations 2005 (SI 2005/79).

10.8 The Licensing Act 2003 (Hearings) (Amendment) Regulations 2005

SI 2005/78

Commencement date: 7 February 2005

These Regulations amend the Licensing Act 2003 (Hearings) Regulations 2005 (SI 2005/44), to correct an omission concerning the provision of a timescale within which a licensing authority must give notice of a hearing to specified persons. The Regulations add a new Regulation 6(4) to the principal Regulations, requiring a licensing authority to give notice of a hearing in cases other than those specified in Regulations 6(2) and 6(3) of the principal Regulations within ten working days before the day, or the first day, of the hearing (Regulation 2).

11 Planning

11.1 Planning and Compulsory Purchase Act 2004

The Planning and Compulsory Purchase Act 2004 received royal assent on 13 May 2004 and will come into force piecemeal on dates set by the Secretary of State.

The aim of the Act is to give effect to the Government's policy on the reform of the planning system set out in the policy statement *Sustainable Communities – Delivering through Planning*, which was published in July 2002. That paper took forward proposals that were outlined in the Green Paper *Planning: Delivering a fundamental change,* published in December 2001. The policy on reform of the compulsory purchase system was set out in the Green Paper daughter document, *Compulsory Purchase and Compensation: delivering a fundamental change*, published in December 2001 and confirmed in the policy statement, *Compulsory Purchase Powers, Procedures and Compensation: the way forward*, published in July 2002.

In relation to Wales, planning is an area in respect of which functions are devolved to the National Assembly for Wales. The Assembly Government published its own consultation paper, *Planning Delivering for Wales*, in January 2002. The Act gives effect to the Assembly Government's policy, formulated in the light of responses to the consultation document, as announced by the Assembly Minister for Environment in November 2002.

The Act consists of nine parts. These are:

Part 1 – Regional functions;

Part 2 – Local development;

Part 3 – Development;

Part 4 – Development control;

Part 5 – Correction of errors;

Part 6 – Wales;

Part 7 – Crown application of Planning Acts;

Part 8 – Compulsory purchase;

Part 9 – Miscellaneous and general.

Part 1: Regional functions

Part 1 applies only to England and provides that there is to be a regional spatial strategy ('RSS') for each region. This will set out the Secretary of State's policies in respect of the development and use of land in the region. It is intended that the RSS will provide a broad development strategy for the region over a 15 or 20-year period. The Secretary of State has exercised the power he has in the Act to prescribe the existing regional planning guidance as the initial RSS (The Town and Country Planning (Initial Regional Spatial Strategy) (England) Regulations 2004).

Responsibility for keeping an RSS under review and monitoring its implementation rests with the body known as the regional planning body ('RPB') for a region. The RPB must seek advice from county councils and other types of authorities with strategic planning expertise about keeping the RSS under review and monitoring its implementation and preparing draft revisions of the RSS, and these authorities must provide the advice. The RPB must prepare a draft revision of the RSS when it appears to be necessary or expedient to do so, or at such time as is prescribed.

Where the RPB decides to prepare different policies for different areas within the region, the detailed proposals must first be made by an authority with strategic planning expertise.

The RPB must prepare, publish and comply with a statement of its policies for involving persons with an interest in preparing draft revisions.

There are general provisions covering the preparation of draft revisions of the RSS, their submission to the Secretary of State and the holding of examinations in public of draft revisions. The Secretary of State has various default powers and may exercise functions of the RPB where there is no such recognised body in a region.

Part 2: Local development

Part 2 which also applies only to England provides for the preparation of local development documents ('LDDs'). These will replace local plans, unitary development plans and structure plans. Every local planning authority must prepare and maintain a local development scheme. A county council, in respect of any part of their area for which there is a district council, must prepare and maintain a minerals and waste development scheme.

These schemes will set out what LDDs the authority will prepare, their timetable for preparation and whether they are to be prepared jointly with one or more other authorities. County councils, in respect of any part of their area for which there is a district council, will be able to participate in the preparation of LDDs concerning matters other than minerals and waste, by entering a joint committee with one or more local planning authorities. LDDs must be prepared in accordance with the relevant scheme and must be in general conformity with the RSS or the spatial development strategy for London, as appropriate.

There are general provisions relating to the preparation, withdrawal, adoption and approval of LDDs and the examination of development plan documents.

Part 3: Development

Part 3 deals with development and updates the definition of the development plan to take account of the changes to the planning system made by the Act.

It also imposes on those with plan-making functions under Parts 1, 2 and 6 a duty to exercise their functions with the objective of contributing to the achievement of sustainable development.

Part 4: Development control

Part 4 deals with development control. Local planning authorities will be able to introduce local permitted development rights by way of local development orders. The Secretary of State will be able to make development orders and regulations prescribing the procedure for making applications for planning permission and certain consents; to prescribe fees and charges for a wider range of planning functions; and set a timetable for 'called in' and recovered appeals and connected decisions.

The period for the duration of planning permissions is reduced from five years to three years. Local authorities will have the power to vary the length of a particular permission.

Local authorities will have power to decline to determine planning applications in certain circumstances. When this power becomes operative will depend on where local authorities meet certain performance targets.

Part 4 also deals with major infrastructure projects in England, in relation to which the Secretary of State – if he considers the development to be of national or regional importance – may direct that a planning application must be referred to him rather than dealt with by the local planning authority.

A new scheme of planning contributions will replace existing provisions relating to planning obligations ('section 106 agreements'). There will be an alternative means for a developer to make a contribution towards services and facilities without a need to negotiate with the local planning authority. There will be two mechanisms for making contributions: the existing negotiated route or an agreement to pay a fixed amount set out in a document drawn up by the local planning authority. Where contributions on their own are insufficient, both mechanisms may be required.

Outline planning permissions will be retained, subject to a few changes. An application for outline permission must be accompanied by a design statement setting out information on matters such as building heights, access, landscape strategy, mix of use and relationship to public space.

This Part of the Act also amends the provisions for simplified planning zones contained in the Town and Country Planning Act 1990 so that they can only be made where the need for such a zone has been identified in the RSS (or, in relation to Wales, where criteria prescribed by the National Assembly are met).

Local planning authorities are provided with a new enforcement power to serve temporary stop notices. It introduces a duty for persons or bodies which are required to be consulted to respond to consultation requests within a specified time. It also brings the creation of additional floor space within buildings under planning control and so will end the loophole regarding mezzanine floors.

Part 5: Correction of errors

Part 5 deals with the correction of errors. The Secretary of State or an inspector may, subject to various conditions, correct errors contained in decision letters where a decision document is issued which contains a correctable error. The Secretary of State or the inspector may correct the letter where he is requested to do so in writing or where he writes to the applicant explaining that he is considering making a correction. The applicant (and, if the applicant is not the owner of the land, the owner of the land as well) must agree to the correction.

Part 6: Wales

Part 6 contains Wales-specific sections. It reforms the development plan system in Wales, where a single-tier system of local government and a uniform pattern of unitary development plans were introduced by the Local Government (Wales) Act 1994. The basic pattern of development plans (to be known as local development plans) is to be retained. Each local planning authority in Wales will be required to prepare a local development plan, to review it at intervals and to revise it as necessary. Local development plans will be simpler, more concise documents than the present unitary development plans and will focus on the authority's objectives for the use and development of land in their area and their general policies for implementing them (but with scope for more detailed policies in key localities).

Procedures for preparing and revising plans will be simplified. Public participation in formulating plans and expedition in taking them through to adoption are to be maximised through community involvement schemes and timetables agreed between the local planning authority and the National Assembly for Wales (or, if agreement cannot be reached, determined by the Assembly). A shift in the focus of an independent examination of the local development plan towards its overall soundness is intended to encourage examinations to become less adversarial. Provision is also made for the National Assembly for Wales to prepare and publish a national spatial plan for Wales (the 'Wales Spatial Plan'), to which local planning authorities will be required to have regard when preparing their plans.

Part 7: Crown application of Planning Acts

Part 7, Chapter 1 (sections 79 to 89) ends Crown immunity in the planning system and makes special provision in relation to certain planning applications by or on behalf of the Crown and in respect of enforcement of planning control in relation to the Crown in England and Wales.

Part 7, Chapter 2 (sections 90 to 98) makes similar substantive provision for the Scottish Planning Acts, as does Chapter 1 for England and Wales. The drafting and terminology may differ from that in Chapter 1 because of differences in the text and terminology of the Scottish legislation.

Part 8: Compulsory purchase

Part 8 amends the existing power of local authorities, joint planning boards and National Park authorities under section 226(1)(a) of the Town and Country Planning Act 1990 to acquire compulsorily land which is suitable for and required in order to secure the carrying out of development, redevelopment or improvement. They will be able to acquire land by compulsory purchase if they think that it will facilitate the carrying out of development, redevelopment or improvement on or in relation to the land, on condition that such acquisition will be of economic, social or environmental benefit to their area.

This Part also amends procedural provisions in the Acquisition of Land Act 1981 for authorising the compulsory purchase of land. A wider category of persons with an interest in land will be entitled to have their objections to the authorisation heard. There is to be a written representations procedure for considering objections to compulsory purchase authorisation when all objectors entitled to be heard consent. There is to be a power to authorise compulsory purchase in stages and, in the case of unopposed compulsory purchase orders which are not made on behalf of a Minister or the National Assembly for Wales for the confirming authority, to transfer its determination to the acquiring authority. Further provisions in this Part enable an acquiring authority to requisition for information as to the ownership and occupation of land in certain cases.

There are also provisions relating to compensation in respect of land that is compulsorily purchased. These set out the date on which property is to be valued for compensation purposes. In addition, a new statutory scheme is introduced which, subject to certain exceptions, provides for 'loss payments' for those owners and occupiers who are not entitled to receive payments under the home loss scheme set out in sections 29 to 33 of the Land Compensation Act 1973.

Part 9: Miscellaneous and general
Part 9 deals with miscellaneous and general issues.

11.2 The Planning and Compulsory Purchase Act 2004 (Commencement No 1) Order 2004

SI 2004/2097

Commencement date: 6 August 2004

This Order brought into force certain provisions of the Planning and Compulsory Purchase Act 2004.

11.3 The Planning and Compulsory Purchase Act 2004 (Commencement No 2, Transitional Provisions and Savings) Order 2004

SI 2004/2202

Commencement date: 28 September 2004

Article 2 of this Order brought into force on 28 September 2004, in relation to England, the following provisions of the Planning and Compulsory Purchase Act 2004 in so far as they are not already in force:

Part 1 (regional functions);

Part 2 (local development);

Section 38 (reference to development plan in any enactment);

Section 39 (sustainable development);

Section 113 (validity of strategies, plans and documents);

Section 114 so far as it relates to Part 2 of the Act (examination of a document or plan is a statutory inquiry);

Section 119(1) (transitional provisions);

Schedule 6, paragraphs 1, 8 to 13, 15, 16(1) and (2), 17 to 19, 21, 22 and 25 (amendments of the planning Acts);

Schedule 7, paragraphs 2, 3, 6, 8, 11(1) to (3), 16, 17, 19(2), 22 and 23 (amendments of other enactments);

Schedule 8 (transitional provisions for Parts 1 and 2 of the Act); and

Schedule 9, so far as it gives effect to the repeals specified in Part 1 of Schedule 1 to this Order.

Article 3 of this Order brought into force on 28 September 2004, in relation to England and Wales, the following provisions of the Act 2004 in so far as they are not already in force:

Part 5 (correction of errors);

Section 117(1) to (7) (interpretation);

Section 118, except subsection (2) so far as it relates to the Town and Country Planning (Scotland) Act 1997 (amendments);

Section 120, except so far as it relates to the Town and Country Planning (Scotland) Act 1997, to the Planning (Listed Building and Conservation Areas)(Scotland) Act and to the Planning (Hazardous Substances) (Scotland) Act 1997 (repeals);

Schedule 6, paragraphs 20, 23, 24 and 26 (amendments of the planning Acts); and

Schedule 9, so far as it gives effect to the repeals specified in Part 2 of Schedule 1 to this Order.

Article 4 of this Order makes transitional and savings provisions for the purposes of the transitional provisions contained in Schedule 8 to the Act and any regulations made pursuant to paragraph 17 of that Schedule, and in respect of the Isles of Scilly.

11.4 The Planning and Compulsory Purchase Act 2004 (Commencement No 3) Order 2004

SI 2004/2593

Commencement date: 31 October 2004

This Order brought into force, on 31 October 2004, Part 8 (compulsory purchase) and section 111(2) (application to the Crown) of the Planning and Compulsory Purchase Act 2004, together with certain consequential amendments in Schedules 6 and 7 and repeals in Schedule 9.

11.5 The Town and Country Planning (Transitional Arrangements) (England) Regulations 2004

SI 2004/2205

Commencement date: 28 September 2004

These Regulations are made under Schedule 8 to the Planning and Compulsory Purchase Act 2004 and make transitional arrangements that will apply as changes to the local development planning system in England are brought into effect.

The development plans to which the transitional arrangements apply are structure plans, unitary development plans and local plans. The Regulations set out the circumstances in which the Town and Country Planning (Development Plan) (England) Regulations 1999 will continue to apply to development plans that are being prepared when the new development planning system comes into force.

The detail of the transitional arrangements is set out in the amendments to the 1999 Regulations that are set out in the Schedule to these Regulations.

11.6 The Town and Country Planning (Regional Planning) (England) Regulations 2004

SI 2004/2203

Commencement date: 28 September 2004

Part 1 of the Planning and Compulsory Purchase Act 2004 establishes a new system of regional development planning in

England. These Regulations make provision for the operation of the regional planning system. The Regulations set out the criteria for the recognition of a Regional Planning Body ('RPB') and regulate its preparation of an annual monitoring report and regional participation statement. They prescribe the form and content of a draft revision of a Regional Spatial Strategy ('RSS') and regulate the procedure to be followed in connection with the preparation of the draft revision. There are also provisions about electronic communications (Regulation 3) and the availability of documents (Part 5).

The main steps in the procedure for the preparation of a draft revision are:

a) consultation with certain bodies prior to the submission of the draft revision to the Secretary of State (Regulation 11);

b) submission to the Secretary of State (Regulation 12);

c) publication of the draft revision and of associated documents, in respect of which representations may be made (Regulation 13);

d) where the Secretary of State decides that an examination in public should be held to consider the draft revision and representations on it, publication of details about the examination (Regulation 14);

e) publication of the report of the person appointed to hold the examination (Regulation 15);

f) publication of any changes the Secretary of State proposes to make to the draft revision, in respect of which representations may be made (Regulation 16);

g) publication of the revised RSS (Regulation 17).

There are also provisions about the procedure to be followed if an RSS is withdrawn by an RPB or the Secretary of State (Regulation

18), and if the Secretary of State prepares a draft revision (Regulation 23).

11.7 The Town and Country Planning (Local Development) (England) Regulations 2004

SI 2004/2204

Commencement date: 28 September 2004

These Regulations prescribe the form and content of the local development scheme to be prepared by local planning authorities ('LPAs') and the procedure to be followed to bring it into effect (Part 3).

The Planning and Compulsory Purchase Act 2004 provides for two forms of local development documents ('LDDs'):

- Supplementary planning documents ('SPDs').

- Development plan documents ('DPDs').

The Regulations prescribe the form and content of LDDs (Part 4) and regulate the procedure to be followed in their preparation.

The main steps in the SPD procedure are:

a) publication of the SPD and consultation with certain bodies about it (Regulation 17);

b) consideration of representations made about the SPD (Regulation 18);

c) adoption of the SPD by the LPA (Regulation 19).

There are also provisions about the withdrawal or revocation of SPDs (Regulations 20 and 21) and the intervention of the Secretary of State in the SPD preparation process (Regulations 22 and 23).

The main steps in the DPD procedure are:

a) publication of the proposals for a DPD and consultation with certain bodies about those proposals (Regulations 25 and 26);

b) consideration of representations made about the DPD proposals (Regulation 27);

c) submission of the DPD to the Secretary of State (Regulation 28);

d) representations made about the DPD (Regulation 29);

e) independent examination of the DPD, including consideration of representations made, by a person appointed by the Secretary of State (Regulation 34);

f) publication of the recommendations of the person appointed to carry out the examination (Regulation 35);

g) adoption of the DPD by the LPA (Regulation 36).

There are also provisions about how different forms of representation on a DPD are to be handled (Regulations 31 and 32), about the withdrawal of a DPD (Regulation 37) and the intervention of the Secretary of State in the DPD preparation process (including provisions about DPDs directed by the Secretary of State to be submitted for his consideration) (Regulations 38 to 45).

The Regulations also make provision for the preparation of joint LDDs (Regulation 46) and the operation of joint committees (comprising two or more local planning authorities) (Regulation 47). They also require the preparation by the LPA of an annual monitoring report (Regulation 48), make provision about electronic communications (Regulation 4) and about the availability of documents (Part 9).

The Regulations apply to county councils for the purposes of minerals and waste development planning as they apply to LPAs for local development planning purposes.

11.8 The Town and Country Planning (Initial Regional Spatial Strategy) (England) Regulations 2004

SI 2004/2206

Commencement date: 28 September 2004

Section 1 of the Planning and Compulsory Purchase Act 2004 provides that for each of the regions (except London) specified in Schedule 1 to the Regional Development Agencies Act 1998, there must be a regional spatial strategy. These Regulations prescribe the regional planning guidance relating to each region which is to be the regional spatial strategy for that region, from the date appointed for the commencement of section 1 of the Planning and Compulsory Purchase Act 2004.

11.9 The Town and Country Planning (Regions) (National Parks) (England) Order 2004

SI 2004/2207

Commencement date: 28 September 2004

Section 12(2) of the Planning and Compulsory Purchase Act 2004 enables the Secretary of State, by order, to direct that if an area of a National Park falls within more than one region of those (except London) specified in Schedule 1 of the Regional Development Agencies Act 1998, it is treated as falling wholly within one of them. This Order directs that the North York Moors National Park and the Yorkshire Dales National Park are treated as falling within the Yorkshire and Humber Region and that the Peak District National Park is treated as falling within the East Midlands Region.

11.10 The Town and Country Planning (Regional Planning Guidance as Revision of Regional Spatial Strategy) Order 2004

SI 2004/2208

Commencement date: 28 September 2004

Section 10(7) of the Planning and Compulsory Purchase Act 2004 provides that section 10(8) of the Act shall apply if any step has been taken in connection with the preparation of any part of regional planning guidance, and the Secretary of State thinks that the step corresponds to a step which must be taken under Part 1 of the Act in connection with the preparation and publication of a revision of the regional spatial strategy. Article 2 of this Order provides that the part of the regional planning guidance set out in the first column of the Schedule to this Order shall have effect as a revision of the regional spatial strategy specified in the second column of that Schedule. The steps taken in the preparation of the regional planning guidance set out in the first column of the Schedule are to be taken as corresponding to the steps that must be taken in connection with the preparation and publication of a revision of the regional spatial strategy, set out in column 2 of the Schedule.

11.11 The Town and Country Planning (Regional Spatial Strategies) (Examinations in Public) (Remuneration and Allowances) (England) Regulations 2004

SI 2004/2209

Commencement date: 28 September 2004

Section 1 of the Planning and Compulsory Purchase Act 2004 provides that there is to be a regional spatial strategy ('RSS') for each region, setting out the Secretary of State's policies in relation to the development and use of land within the region. Each region's RSS is reviewed by the regional planning body, which may prepare a draft revision of the RSS for submission to the Secretary of State. On receipt of a draft revision, the Secretary of State may decide that an examination in public should be held into the draft revision. Where he decides to do so, the examination must be held before a person appointed by the Secretary of State. These Regulations provide for remuneration and allowances to be payable to such appointed persons by the Secretary of State. Regulation 2 provides that the appointed person may be paid £342 for each day he is engaged on the examination in public or work connected with it. Regulations 3 and 4, to which the Schedule is relevant, provide the rates of travelling and subsistence allowances payable to the appointed persons.

11.12 The Planning (Listed Buildings and Conservation Areas) (Amendment) (England) Regulations 2004

SI 2004/2210

Commencement date: 28 September 2004

These Regulations amend the Planning (Listed Buildings and Conservation Areas) Regulations 1990. Most of the amendments are consequential on amendments and repeals in the Planning and Compulsory Purchase Act 2004. They insert publicity requirements for applications for planning permission for development which the local planning authority think will affect the setting of a listed building, or the character or appearance of a conservation area.

Different publicity requirements, in relation to such applications and applications for listed building consent and conservation area consent, apply to applications made to the Council of the London Borough of Camden. In the case of that authority, there is no requirement to advertise those applications in a newspaper. Instead, the authority is required to advertise the applications by site notice and to place a notice of the application on a website maintained for the purpose of advertisement of applications. This brings the publicity requirement provisions for these applications made to the London Borough of Camden into line with the provisions contained in the Town and Country Planning (London Borough of Camden) Special Development Order 2004 (SI 2004/1704), which exempts Camden from the requirement to publicise applications for planning permission in a local newspaper, with the exception of applications that require environmental impact assessment.

11.13 The Local Authorities (Functions and Responsibilities) (Amendment) (No 2) (England) Regulations 2004

SI 2004/2211

Commencement date: 28 Septeber 2004

These Regulations amend the Local Authorities (Functions and Responsibilities) (England) Regulations 2000. Regulation 2 amends Schedule 1 (functions not to be the responsibility of the authority's executive) of the 2000 Regulations by the substitution of a new paragraph A. The amendments are concerned with functions under Part 2 of the Planning and Compulsory Purchase Act 2004, which relate to development plan documents and joint committees that are, or are to be (for the purposes of that Part), local planning authorities. The provisions relating to these functions came into force on 28 September 2004 by virtue of the Planning and Compulsory Purchase Act 2004 (Commencement No. 2, Transitional Provisions and Savings) Order 2004 (SI 2004/2202).

11.14 The Transport and Works (Inquiries Procedure) Rules 2004

SI 2004/2018

Commencement date: 23 August 2004

These Rules prescribe the procedure to be followed in connection with public local inquiries held under section 11 of the Transport and Works Act 1992. These relate to applications for orders under Part I of the 1992 Act authorising:

a) the construction or operation of railways, tramways, trolley vehicle systems and other systems of guided transport (as prescribed under section 2 of the 1992 Act) and matters ancillary thereto;

b) the construction and operation of inland waterways and matters ancillary thereto;

c) the carrying out of certain works which interfere with navigation and have been prescribed pursuant to section 4 of the 1992 Act.

The Rules extend to England and Wales. They replace, with amendments, and revoke subject to transitional provisions, the Transport and Works (Inquiries Procedure) Rules 1992 (SI 1992/2817).

11.15 The Planning and Compulsory Purchase Act 2004 (Commencement No 1 and Transitional Provision) (Wales) Order 2004

SI 2004/1814

Commencement date: 14 July 2004

Section 60 of the Planning and Compulsory Purchase Act 2004 imposes on the National Assembly for Wales the duty to prepare a spatial plan, to consult the public on its provisions and to approve and publish it. Article 2 of this Order brought section 60 into force on 14 July 2004.

Work on the preparation of the Wales Spatial Plan, including public consultation, having been begun under the National Assembly's general powers prior to the coming into force of section 60, Article 3 of this Order provides that steps taken by the National Assembly in relation to that plan before that section came into force are, nevertheless, to be regarded as steps taken pursuant to the relevant duties under that section.

11.16 The Planning and Compulsory Purchase Act 2004 (Commencement No 2) (Wales) Order 2004

SI 2004/1813

Commencement date: 1 August 2004

This Order brought certain provisions of Part 6 (Wales) of the Planning and Compulsory Purchase Act 2004 into force on the 1

August 2004. Part 6 establishes, in Wales, a system of local development plans in place of the unitary development plans required under Chapter I of Part II of the Town and Country Planning Act 1990. The effect of the Order is to enable the National Assembly for Wales to make regulations and to give guidance to local planning authorities in Wales in preparation for the coming into force of the new system of development plans, which will take place at a later date.

Section 62(4) empowers the National Assembly to prescribe, by regulations, the form and content of plans.

Section 62(5)(g) empowers the National Assembly to prescribe, by regulations, matters additional to those listed in subsection (5) to which local planning authorities must have regard when preparing a plan.

Section 63 provides for community involvement schemes, which will state the authority's policy for involving certain persons in the exercise of the authority's functions under Part 6. Section 63(3)(a) empowers the National Assembly to prescribe, by regulations, who those persons are to include.

Section 63(7) of the Act empowers the National Assembly to prescribe, by regulations, various matters relating to the preparation of plans.

Section 75 requires authorities, when exercising any function conferred under or by virtue of Part 6, to have regard to any guidance issued by the National Assembly.

Section 76(2) requires annual monitoring reports made by authorities under subsection (1) to include such information as is prescribed by the National Assembly by regulations.

Section 76(3) requires annual monitoring reports to be made at such times, in such form and including such information as is prescribed by the National Assembly by regulations.

Section 77 empowers the National Assembly, by regulations, to make provision in relation to the exercise of functions under Part 6 and, in particular, to make provision in relation to the matters listed in section 77(2).

Section 78 defines terms used in Part 6 of the Act.

11.17 The Town and Country Planning (General Development Procedure) (Amendment) (England) Order 2004

SI 2004/3340

Commencement date: 14 January 2005

This Order, which applies in relation to England only, amends the Town and Country Planning (General Development Procedure) Order 1995 by altering the time limit for appeals from three to six months.

11.18 The Planning (Listed Buildings and Conservation Areas) (Amendment) (No 2) (England) Regulations 2004

SI 2004/3341

Commencement date: 14 January 2005

These Regulations, which apply in relation to England only, amend Regulation 8 of, and Parts I, II and III of Schedule 1 to, the Planning (Listed Buildings and Conservation Areas) Regulations 1990 by altering the time limit for appeals from three to six months.

11.19 The Planning and Compulsory Purchase Act 2004 (Commencement No 4 and Savings) Order 2005

SI 2005/204

Commencement date: 7 March 2005 and 1 April 2005

Article 2 of this Order brought into force, on 7 March 2005, in relation to England, section 52 (temporary stop notice) and section

53 (fees and charges) of the Planning and Compulsory Purchase Act 2004, in so far as they are not already in force.

Article 3 of this Order brought into force, on 1 April 2005, in relation to England, section 55 (time in which Secretary of State to take decisions) and Schedule 2 (timetable for decisions) of the Act, in so far as they are not already in force.

Article 4 of this Order makes a saving for the purposes of the provisions contained in Schedule 2 to the Act.

11.20 The Town and Country Planning (Timetable for Decisions) (England) Order 2005

SI 2005/205

Commencement date: 1 April 2005

Schedule 2 to the Planning and Compulsory Purchase Act 2004 requires the Secretary of State to make timetables for the purposes of decisions to which that Schedule applies, and enables him by order to specify decisions or descriptions of decision to which a timetable is not to apply. This Order specifies those descriptions of decision.

11.21 The Town and Country Planning (Temporary Stop Notice) (England) Regulations 2005

SI 2005/206

Commencement date: 7 March 2005

Section 171E of the Town and Country Planning Act 1990 enables a local planning authority to issue a temporary stop notice if they think that there has been a breach of planning control and that it is expedient that the activity – or any part of it – which amounts to the breach, is stopped immediately.

Section 171F(1)(a) provides that a temporary stop notice does not prohibit the use of a building as a dwellinghouse. Section 171F(1)(b) enables the Secretary of State to prescribe descriptions of activities which are not prohibited by a temporary stop notice, and circumstances in which the carrying out of an activity is not prohibited by a temporary stop notice.

Regulation 2 of these Regulations prescribes, for the purposes of section 171(1)(b), the stationing of a caravan on land where the land is used for that purpose immediately before the issue of the temporary stop notice, and the caravan is at that time occupied by a person as his main residence. This applies unless the local planning authority consider that the risk of harm to a compelling public interest arising from the stationing of the caravan is so serious as to outweigh any benefit to the occupier of the caravan in the stationing of the caravan for the period for which the temporary stop notice has effect.

These Regulations apply in relation to England only.

11.22 The Town and Country Planning (Use Classes) (Amendment) (England) Order 2005

SI 2005/84

Commencement date: 21 April 2005

This Order amends the Town and Country Planning (Use Classes) Order 1987. The 1987 Order specifies classes for the purposes of section 55(2)(f) of the Town and Country Planning Act 1990, which provides that a change of use of a building or other land does not involve development, for the purposes of the Act, if the new use and the former use are both within the same specified class.

This Order amends the 1987 Order, by excluding from the specified classes use as a retail warehouse club and use as a nightclub. It also has the effect of including use as an internet café in the shops class

(Class A1), and splitting the former A3 use class (food and drink), into three new classes: Class A3 (use as a restaurant or café), Class A4 (use as a public house, wine-bar or other drinking establishment) and Class A5 (use as a hot food takeaway).

11.23 The Town and Country Planning (General Permitted Development) (Amendment) (England) Order 2005

SI 2005/85

Commencement date: 21 April 2005

This Order amends the Town and Country Planning (General Permitted Development) Order 1995. Part 3 of Schedule 2 to that Order grants planning permission for certain changes of use by reference to classes of use specified in the Town and Country Planning (Use Classes) Order 1987 (SI 1987/764). That Order is amended by the Town and Country Planning (Use Classes) (Amendment) (England) Order 2005, which substitutes for the former class A3 (food and drink) three new use classes: restaurants and cafés (A3), drinking establishments (A4) and hot food takeaways (A5).

Article 2 of this Order, which amends Part 3 of Schedule 2 to the 1995 Order, reflects the three new use classes which replace the former class A3 (food and drink). The three new use classes are given permitted development rights to change to shops (A1) uses or financial and professional services (A2) uses specified in the 1987 Order.

Drinking establishments and hot food takeaways are given permitted development rights to change to restaurants and cafés.

Article 2 has the effect of removing the permitted development rights for motor car showrooms to change to shops (A1) uses.

12 Probate

12.1 The Non-Contentious Probate Fees Order 2004

SI 2004/3120

Commencement date: 4 January 2005

This Order replaces the Non-Contentious Probate Fees Order 1999 (SI 1999/688) which specified fees for non-contentious probate matters in the principal registry and district registries. It incorporates amendments to that Order since 1999 and includes some fee changes:

- The fee for the application for a grant (or for resealing a grant) where the assessed value of the estate exceeds £5,000 has been reduced from £50 to £40.

- The Personal application fee, where the assessed value of the estate exceeds £5,000, has been reduced from £80 to £50.

12.2 The Inheritance Tax (Delivery of Accounts) (Excepted Estates) Regulations 2004

SI 2004/2543

Commencement date: 1 November 2004

These Regulations replace the Inheritance Tax (Delivery of Accounts) (Excepted Estates) Regulations 2002 (SI 2002/1733) ('the 2002 Regulations') in relation to estates of persons who died on or after 6 April 2004. The 2002 Regulations and these new Regulations make provision in relation to the delivery of accounts and other information for inheritance tax purposes. These Regulations make some new and different provisions, which are noted below.

Regulation 1 provides for citation, commencement and effect.

Regulation 2 interprets some of the terms used in the Regulations.

Regulation 3 provides that a person is not required to deliver an account for inheritance tax purposes under section 216 of the Inheritance Tax Act 1984 ('the 1984 Act') of property comprised in an excepted estate. This Regulation also includes a new provision in relation to estates which no longer qualify as an excepted estate following the alteration of the dispositions taking effect on death within section 142 of the 1984 Act.

Regulation 4 defines an excepted estate. There are three categories of excepted estate; these are as follows. The first category is where the aggregate of the gross value of the estate and the value of certain lifetime transfers of a person domiciled in the United Kingdom does not exceed a certain amount, determined by either the inheritance tax nil rate band for the year in which death occurred or the previous year. This is based on the first category of excepted estates in the 2002 Regulations but differs in the following respects. First, the limit on the aggregate of the gross value of the deceased estate and the value transferred by certain lifetime transfers is directly linked to the inheritance tax nil rate band. Second, as in the 2002 Regulations, the lifetime transfers to be taken into account include specified transfers which are defined, but the definition differs in these Regulations, as the property which may be transferred is extended to include personal chattels and corporeal moveable property. Third, in valuing specified transfers, the Regulations now provide that business property relief and agricultural property relief in sections 104 and 116 of the 1984 Act shall not apply. Finally, a new class of lifetime transfer which must be taken into account is introduced in these Regulations, which are defined as specified exempt transfers.

The second category is a new category of excepted estate introduced in these Regulations, where the aggregate of the gross value of the estate and the value of certain lifetime transfers of a person domiciled in the United Kingdom does not exceed £1,000,000, and that aggregate value after deduction of liabilities and the value of any spouse and charity transfers made on death does not exceed the inheritance tax nil rate band.

The third category is where the deceased was never domiciled or treated as domiciled in the United Kingdom and his estate in the United Kingdom consists only of cash or quoted shares or securities with a gross value not exceeding £100,000. This is the same as the equivalent provision in the 2002 Regulations.

Regulations 5, 6 and 7 are new provisions.

Regulation 5 defines spouse and charity transfer.

Regulation 6 specifies the information that must be produced to the Board of Inland Revenue in the case of excepted estates and Regulation 7 specifies to whom it must be produced.

Regulations 8 and 9 provide for the discharge of persons and property from tax in relation to property comprised in an excepted estate. Regulation 8 differs from the equivalent provision in the 2002 Regulations to reflect the fact that specified information must now be produced to the Board for excepted estates. Regulation 9 is the same as the equivalent provision in the 2002 Regulations.

Regulation 10 makes provision for excepted estates in relation to transfers reported late under section 264 of the Inheritance Tax Act 1984. This has the same effect as the equivalent provision in the 2002 Regulations.

Regulation 11 revokes the Inheritance Tax (Delivery of Accounts) (Excepted Estates) Regulations 2002 (SI 2002/1733) and the Inheritance Tax (Delivery of Accounts) (Excepted Estates) (Amendment) Regulations 2003 (SI 2003/1688) in relation to persons who died on or after 6 April 2004.

13   Rights of way

13.1 The Countryside and Rights of Way Act 2000 (Commencement No 5) (Wales) Order 2004

SI 2004/1489

Commencement date: 21 June 2004

This Order brought into force, on 21 June 2004, sections 18, 20 and 46(1)(a) of – and, in so far as it relates to the repeal of section 193(2) of the Law of Property Act 1925, Part I of Schedule 16 to – the Countryside and Rights of Way Act 2000.

13.2 The Countryside and Rights of Way Act 2000 (Commencement No 6) Order 2004

SI 2004/3088

Commencement date: 14 December 2004

This Order brought into force, on 14th December 2004, section 2 of the Countryside and Rights of Way Act 2000 (which introduces a new right of access to access land) in so far as it relates to access land which is shown as open country or registered common land on a map in conclusive form, and which lies within an area covered by the map in conclusive form issued by the Countryside Agency on 28 September 2004 (such map relates to the central southern area of England).

The Order also brought into force section 2 in so far as it relates to access land which is dedicated as access land under section 16 of the Countryside and Rights of Way Act 2000, which is not also shown as open country or registered common land on a map in conclusive form, but which lies within an area covered by the map in conclusive form issued on 28 September 2004. The day appointed for section 2 in relation to such land is 14 December

2004, or the end of a period of six months beginning with the day on which the land is dedicated under section 16, whichever is the later.

14   Stamp Duty Land Tax

14.1 The Stamp Duty Land Tax (Appeals) Regulations 2004

SI 2004/1363

Commencement date: 11 June 2004

These Regulations make provision for appeals and other proceedings, which will be determined by the Commissioners in relation to Stamp Duty Land Tax.

14.2 The Stamp Duty Land Tax (Amendment of Part 4 of the Finance Act 2003) Regulations 2004

SI 2004/1069

Commencement date: 7 April 2004

These Regulations amend Part 4 of the Finance Act 2003, to make further provision in respect of the computation of chargeable consideration in respect of land transactions involving public or educational bodies.

14.3 The Stamp Duty Land Tax (Amendment of Part 4 of the Finance Act 2003) (No 2) Regulations 2004

SI 2004/1206

Commencement date: 27 April 2004

These Regulations amend paragraph 17(1)(b) of Schedule 4 to the Finance Act 2003 so that it refers to a lease back of land by a non-qualifying body to a qualifying body. This substitution corrects an error made in SI 2004/1069.

14.4 The Stamp Duty Land Tax (Administration) (Amendment) Regulations 2004

SI 2004/3124

Commencement date: 6 December 2004

These Regulations amend the Stamp Duty Land Tax (Administration) Regulations 2003 (SI 2003/2837), to substitute a new prescribed form in Part 4 of Schedule 2 to those Regulations for the purpose of a land transaction return. The Regulations make transitional provision so that, until 31 March 2005, either the form prescribed by them, or the form which it replaces, may be used.

14.5 The Stamp Duty Land Tax (Consequential Amendment of Enactments) Regulations 2005

SI 2005/82

Commencement date: 11 February 2005

These Regulations make amendments consequent upon the introduction of Stamp Duty Land Tax. In this respect they replace provision made for the treatment of NHS trusts by SI 2003/2687. They also make provision for the disclosure of information to the Commissioner of Valuation for Northern Ireland.

Regulation 2 substitutes a new subsection (3) in section 61 of the National Health Service and Community Care Act 1990. Section 33(2) of the Health and Social Care (Community Health and Standards) Act 2003 applied the existing section 61(3) to foundation trusts as it applied to other NHS trusts. As substituted, subsection (3) re-enacts the exemption from stamp duty for instruments effecting conveyances, leases and transfers in favour of certain health service bodies. It also provides a similar exemption from Stamp Duty Land Tax, in respect of land transactions where the purchaser is a health service body, thus enabling a foundation trust to take the benefit of the exemption from Stamp Duty Land

Tax. Subsection (3A) lists the health service bodies to which subsection (3) applies. Subsection (3B) specifies the method of claiming relief under subsection (3)(b), and subsection (3C) defines terms used in subsection (3).

Regulation 3 amends Part 6 of the Finance Act 1994. The amendment made to section 245 of that Act provides that information received by the Commissioners of Inland Revenue in respect of stamp duty land transaction returns may be disclosed to the Commissioner of Valuation for Northern Ireland in the same way as particulars delivered under section 244 of the 1994 Act.

Regulation 4 repeals section 61A of the 1990 Act, which was inserted by SI 2003/2867. Regulation 5 revokes the provision in SI 2003/2867 which inserted section 61A of the 1990 Act.

Part C

OTHER RECENT DEVELOPMENTS

1   *FREEDOM OF INFORMATION*

The Freedom of Information Act 2000, which came into force on 1 January 2005, provides a right of access to recorded information held by public authorities, such as government departments and agencies, local authorities, and even some publicly owned companies. The Act also creates exemptions from the duty to disclose information and establishes arrangements for enforcement and appeal. Its aim is to transform the culture of government from one of secrecy to one of openness.

The Act enables anyone to ask a public authority whether it holds specified information, and to have that information communicated to him free of charge (unless the cost of providing that information exceeds £450, or £600 in the case of requests for information from central government departments).

The new regime will affect any business that has – or has had – dealings with public bodies. It applies to information belonging to public bodies and to any information about external organisations in their possession. The Act will affect contracts with public bodies, information contained in tender and other documents, and will apply retrospectively to all the information they possess.

A public authority will not have to disclose information where an exemption applies. These fall into two specific types:

a) Absolute exemption

Although there are eight categories of information to which an absolute exemption applies, perhaps the most relevant for commercial businesses is 'confidential information'. Under this category, an absolute exemption applies if the requested information was provided to the public authority in confidence, i.e. if the information was disclosed by the public authority, the disclosure would be an actionable breach of confidence by the public authority.

The following factors are relevant in determining whether an obligation of confidence has arisen:

- the circumstances under which information was provided to the public authority; and

- whether the information has the necessary 'quality of confidence', i.e. it must not be trivial, nor must it be readily available by other means.

Companies will need to be very precise about what is marked as confidential; the simple marking of documents with words such as 'confidential' will not necessarily ensure that the information will fall within the exemption, as the information may not actually have the necessary 'quality of confidence'.

The Information Commissioner has advised that public authorities should set out formally the circumstances under which it would regard information as confidential. It has also advised that public authorities should refuse to include contractual terms that purport generally to restrict the disclosure of information held by the authority.

b) Qualified exemption

There are 16 categories of information that will only class an exemption if, in all the circumstances of the case, the public interest in maintaining the exemption outweighs the public interest in disclosing the information (the 'public interest test').

The one of most concern to businesses will be that of 'commercially sensitive information'. Information will be commercially sensitive if it constitutes a trade secret; or its disclosure would, or would be likely to, prejudice the commercial interests of any person (including the public authority) and the public interest in not disclosing the information outweighs the public interest in disclosing it.

If the information is used for the 'purpose of trade', or if it is obvious that the owner would regard the release of the information to be commercially advantageous to rivals, this may constitute a trade secret.

'Commercial interests' is a wider concept, relating to a person's ability to successfully participate in a commercial activity. In deciding whether the release of such information would prejudice someone's commercial interests, it would be necessary to consider all of the surrounding circumstances.

A business which wants to protect sensitive information could ask the public body not to disclose the relevant information or, if that fails, seek an injunction to prevent disclosure. However, the Act does not concern itself with the interests of anyone who may be affected by requests for information and does not require public bodies to inform third parties on receipt of a request for information, or to consult with third parties about whether to provide the information, or to obtain their consent before doing so.

Businesses will need to think carefully about how to manage the risks of information becoming public. Any public interest in keeping information confidential is likely to diminish as that information becomes dated and the changes made by the Act will make it very difficult for businesses to keep information held by public bodies out of the public gaze indefinitely.

The Information Commissioner and the Department for Constitutional Affairs have published guidance on the Act, including guidance on 'confidential information', 'commercially sensitive information' and on the public interest test. The Lord Chancellor has published a Code of Practice which sets out the standard public authorities are expected to meet in order to comply with their obligations. The Code also provides guidance on the procedures for complaint that public authorities should follow.

2   ASBESTOS

Regulation 4 of the Control of Asbestos at Work Regulations 2002 (SI 2002 No. 2675) came into force on 21 May 2004. It introduced a new legal duty to manage asbestos in non-domestic property and is in addition to the duties which exist under the Control of Asbestos at Work Regulations 1987.

The duty is imposed on anyone who has responsibility for maintenance activities in non-domestic property, for example landlords, tenants and licensees. Those subject to the duty are required:

● To assess whether there is any asbestos in the property, which will entail keeping a written register of any actual or suspected asbestos in a building.

● To decide whether to remove it or to manage it.

● To ensure that, if there is asbestos in the property and it is decided not to remove it, workers carrying out maintenance are not exposed to avoidable risk. This will involve a risk assessment and implementation of a risk management plan.

3   STANDARD COMMERCIAL PROPERTY CONDITIONS

The second edition of the Standard Commercial Property Conditions came into effect on 1 June 2004. The second edition takes account of the changes made by the Land Registration Act 2002, Part I of the Commonhold and Leasehold Reform Act 2002, and a number of other developments. The Standard Commercial Property Conditions are intended primarily for use in more complex commercial transactions, as appears in particular from the extended provisions they contain in relation to leasehold matters, VAT and capital allowances. For residential sales and sales of small business premises, the Standard Conditions of Sale (Fourth Edition) will be better suited.

The Standard Commercial Property Conditions are now divided into two parts:

Part 1 contains conditions of general application and is an updated and expanded version of the first edition.

Part 2 comprises new conditions relating to VAT, capital allowances and reversionary interests in flats.

The conditions in Part 1 apply, except as varied or excluded by the contract (1.1.4(a)), but a condition in Part 2 applies only if expressly incorporated (1.1.4(b)).

The second edition of the Standard Commercial Property Conditions of Sale is available from Oyez Forms Publishing (020 7232 1000), Everyform (www.everyform.net) and Laserform (01925 750000).

4   PRIVATE SEWERS AND DRAINS IN ENGLAND AND WALES

In October 2004, the Government published its response to its 2003 consultation seeking views on a number of possible solutions to the difficulties surrounding private sewers and drains, including the adoption of private sewers by sewerage undertakers. The response summarises the responses and gives the Government's views, as well as issues that need to be addressed before a final decision can be made. There is already a protocol for the construction of new

153

sewers. All sewers are to be built to a standard that would not preclude their adoption by the sewerage undertaker, and new legislation will allow sewerage undertakers to adopt laterals (that part of the drain situated outside a property boundary and running from the boundary to the sewer) if they are built to an adoptable standard. The aim of the protocol is to put into practice a common approach for the design and construction for new development, to enable wider adoption of sewers in England and Wales. Details of hydraulic design and minimum pipe size that should form part of a common standard are given. The documents can be found at www.defra.gov.uk.

5   RATES

The Valuation Office Agency has published details of new rateable values for 2005-10. The new rateable values will form the basis of rates bills issued in April 2005. The new rateable values have been published online, at www.voa.gov.uk, to allow businesses to compare their assessments with those of their neighbours and competitors. The Office of the Deputy Prime Minister has also announced proposals to streamline the appeals process. Further details are available at www.odpm.gov.uk.

6   COMPULSORY PURCHASE ORDERS

The Law Commission's report (LC291) on the procedure relating to compulsory purchase orders was published on 15 December 2004 and is available at www.lawcom.gov.uk.

7   THE 1954 ACT REFORMS

Changes to Part II of the Landlord and Tenant Act 1954 took effect from 1 June 2004 with the aim to simplify the contracting-out process and to modernise and streamline the Act.

The principal changes are as follows:

- Landlords and tenants no longer need to ask the courts to authorise agreements to exclude business leases from the protection of the Act or to authorise agreements to surrender business leases. The parties are now able to enter into agreements to exclude the Act either before the tenant becomes contractually bound by a lease, or by any preceding agreement for lease, or by an agreement for surrender if the landlord has served a warning notice on the tenant and the tenant has made a declaration confirming that it accepts the consequences of contracting out of the Act.

- The common law rule in *Esselte AB v Pearl Assurance plc* – that tenants can vacate the premises before the contractual expiry of the term, without serving any prior notice on the landlord – is now on a statutory footing.

- Tenants can bring continuation tenancies to an end by giving three months' notice to end on any day, rather than on a quarter day, and will be entitled to an apportionment and refund of any consequential overpayment of rent.

- Landlords and tenants are able to serve section 40 notices on each other during the last two years of the lease requesting information regarding occupancy and ownership. Both are obliged to respond and to update that information for six months afterwards, otherwise they will be liable in damages.

- Landlords have to set out their proposals for any new tenancy in their section 25 notices.

- The requirement that a tenant must serve a counter-notice in response to a landlord's section 25 notice has been abolished, but the requirement that a landlord must serve a counter-notice in response to a tenant's section 26 request has been retained.

- Landlords and tenants are able to apply to the court for the renewal of a tenancy. Landlords are also able to apply for an order to determine a tenancy, without renewal.

- Landlords and tenants are able to make court applications before the date specified in the landlord's section 25 notice or in the tenant's section 26 request.

- Landlords and tenants are able to extend the deadline for making an application to the court by an agreement made in writing before the deadline imposed by the Act or before the expiry of any previous extension agreement.

- Landlords and tenants are both able to ask the court to determine an interim rent. Interim rent will be payable from the earliest date for termination that could have been specified in the landlord's section 25 notice or in the tenant's section 26 request. Tenants who are granted unopposed new leases of the same premises will usually have to pay the full market rent for their premises during the interim period.

- The maximum length of lease that the court can award is now 15 years.

- Notices served before 1 June 2004 will be subject to the old rules. Landlords and tenants who serve section 25 notices or 26 requests on or after 1 June will be subject to the new regime.

- There are new forms of section 25 notices.

Consequent changes to Part 56 of the Civil Procedure Rules, to take account of the reforms, have been made by the Civil Procedure (Amendment) Rules 2004.

The Office of Deputy Prime Minister has published guidance, *Business Tenancies: new procedures under the Landlord and Tenant Act 1954, Part 2*. This is available for download at

www.odpm.gov.uk/stellent/groups/odpm_urbanpolicy/documents/
page/odpm_urbpol_028212.pdf.

8   *TERRORISM INSURANCE*

The Chapter I prohibition in the Competition Act 1998 affects
agreements, decisions and concerted practices which have the
object or effect of preventing, restricting or distorting competition
in, and which may affect trade within, the UK (or any part of it). The
Office of Fair Trading can grant an individual exemption from the
Chapter I prohibition and, in 2004, issued a consultation paper
requesting views on whether Pool Reinsurance Company Ltd's
arrangements for providing terrorism cover in the United Kingdom
should be exempted from the prohibition. It has concluded that the
rules – requiring members to offer terrorism cover only in conjunction
with general cover for commercial property and to reinsure all their
terrorism insurance for commercial property with Pool Re, and for
policy-holders who buy terrorism insurance for a commercial
property to buy cover for their entire portfolio of commercial
properties – do appreciably restrict or distort competition within the
United Kingdom, but that the benefits of the rules, which ensure
that owners of commercial properties can insure against terrorism
and will help businesses to survive a terrorist act, outweigh their
anti-competitive effects, and has granted Pool Re an exemption.

9   *PLANNING POLICY STATEMENTS*

The ODPM is replacing planning policy guidance notes with shorter
planning policy statements. Further details are available at
www.odpm.gov.uk. So far it has published the following planning
policy statements:

a) PPS 1: Delivering Sustainable Development
PPS 1 sets out the Government's overarching planning policies on

the delivery of sustainable development through the planning system. This PPS replaces *Planning Policy Guidance Note 1 General Policies and Principles* published in February 1997.

b) PPS 7: Sustainable Development in Rural Areas

This Statement replaces PPG 7. It sets out the Government's planning policies for rural areas, which local authorities should have regard to when preparing local development documents and when taking planning decisions.

The main Government objectives are:

- To raise the quality of life and environment in rural areas.

- To promote more sustainable patterns of development.

- To promote the economic performance of the English regions and to promote sustainable, diverse and adaptable agricultural sectors.

The Government's overall aim is to protect the countryside for its own sake. There is still special protection for the best and most versatile agricultural land (grades 1, 2 and 3a), although farm diversification is supported, as are sustainable tourism and leisure developments and facilities.

The key policies are as follows:

- Development proposals should ensure social inclusion, protection of the environment, prudent use of natural resources and should maintain high and stable levels of economic growth and employment.

- Accessibility should be a key consideration in all development decisions; good quality accessible development within existing towns and villages should be allowed where it benefits the local economy and/or community (e.g. affordable housing for identified local needs).

- New development in the open countryside, away from existing settlements or outside allocated areas, should be strictly controlled – although the reuse and replacement of existing buildings is permitted subject to certain criteria, and priority should be given to the reuse of brownfield sites.

- New development should focus on local service centres identified in the development plan, but limited development should be allowed in non-designated rural settlements in order to meet local business and community needs.

- The special justification for houses of exceptional quality is retained.

- Major developments should not take place in specially designated areas (for example national parks), except in exceptional circumstances.

c) PPS 11: Regional Spatial Strategies

Part 1 of the Planning and Compulsory Purchase Act 2004 replaces regional planning guidance with regional spatial strategies. For each region there is to be a regional spatial strategy which must set out the Secretary of State's policies in relation to the development and use of the land in that region. The RSS will then form part of the statutory development plan. PPS 11 sets out the relevant procedural policy for these.

d) PPS 12: Local Development Frameworks

This replaces PPG 12 Development Plans, though PPG 12 will remain in operation for development plans still being prepared under the 1999 Development Plan Regulations. Under Part 2 of the Planning and Compulsory Purchase Act 2004, local plans and unitary development plans are replaced by local development frameworks. The Act does not specifically refer to LDFs, rather it focuses on their constituent parts. An LDF will comprise a series of local development documents. Some of these will have development plan status, while others will be the equivalent of supplementary planning guidance. PPS 12 sets out the relevant procedural policy.

e) PPS 22: Renewable Energy

PPS 22 sets out the Government policy on renewable energy and replaces PPG 22.

The main Government objectives were set out in the Energy White Paper, with the principal aim to reduce carbon dioxide emissions by 60% by 2050. The target is to generate 10% of electricity from renewable sources by 2010, with the aspiration to achieve 20% by 2020.

The key policies are as follows:

- Renewable energy should be accommodated throughout England.

- Plans should promote and encourage, not restrict, development of renewal energy.

- The criteria to be applied in assessing applications for renewable energy projects should be set out.

- The wider environmental economic benefits of all proposals, whatever their scale, are material and should be given significant weight.

- Planning authorities should not make assumptions about technical and commercial feasibility.

- Small-scale projects can provide a limited but valuable contribution.

Regional strategies should include targets for renewable energy capacity in each region, including any indication of what might be achieved offshore (although these are not covered by land use planning). Offshore generation should not be used as a justification to set lower targets onshore.

Specific sites should only be allocated in plans where a developer has already indicated an interest in the site and has confirmed it is viable. Incorporating renewal energy projects in all new developments should be considered, and authorities may require percentages of energy used in residential, commercial or industrial developments to come from on-site renewable sources. In addition, authorities should not use a sequential approach to identify sites since renewable energy resources can only be developed where the resource exists. Cumulative impact is relevant but arbitrary limits should not be set.

Renewable energy requirements should not override protection for sites of national and international importance, save in exceptional cases. Buffer zones around these protected sites should not, however, be created, nor should local designations be used in themselves to refuse planning permission. In assessing planning applications for wind turbines, authorities should recognise that the impact will vary according to the size and number of turbines and type of landscape involved and that the impact may be temporary if future decommissioning is required.

f) PPS 23: Planning and Pollution Control

This PPS replaces PPG 23 Planning and Pollution Control published in 1994. Waste Planning, including operations under the Waste Management Licensing Regulations 1994 and the Pollution Prevention and Control Regulations 2000, in so far as they apply to waste management, is now dealt with in PPG 10 Planning and Waste Management (September 1999), which is currently under review. Noise is covered by PPG 24 Planning and Noise (1994). The impacts of transport on pollution will be covered in more detail in the forthcoming review of PPG 13 Transport (2001).

This statement advises that:

- Any consideration of the quality of land, air or water and potential impacts arising from development, possibly leading to impacts on health, is capable of being a material planning consideration, in so far as it arises, or may arise from or may affect, any land use.

- The planning system plays a key role in determining the location of development which may give rise to pollution, either directly or indirectly, and in ensuring that other uses and developments are not, as far as possible, affected by major existing or potential sources of pollution.

- The controls under the planning and pollution control regimes should complement rather than duplicate each other.

- The presence of contamination in land can present risks to human health and to the environment, which adversely affect or restrict the beneficial use of land; however, development presents an opportunity to deal with these risks successfully.

- Contamination is not restricted to land with previous industrial uses; it can occur on greenfield sites as well as previously developed land and it can arise from natural sources as well as from human activities.

- Where pollution issues are likely to arise, intending developers should hold informal pre-application discussions with the LPA, the relevant pollution control authority and/or the environmental health departments of local authorities (LAs), as well as with other authorities and stakeholders with a legitimate interest.

- Where it will save time and money, consideration should be given to submitting applications for planning permission and pollution control permits in parallel and co-ordinating their consideration by the relevant authorities.

10 PLANNING FACTSHEETS

On 17 June 2004, the ODPM published the following planning factsheets:

Planning Factsheet 1: Privacy and Overlooking;
Planning Factsheet 2: External Lighting;
Planning Factsheet 3: Overshadowing.

Further details are available at www.odpm.gov.uk.

11 COMMONHOLD GUIDANCE

The Department of Constitutional Affairs has issued guidance, *Commonhold: Guidance on the drafting of a Commonhold Community Statement including Specimen Local Rules*, on using voluntary clauses in the Commonhold Community Statement. This guidance will provide useful precedents, and the model worked example of a Commonhold Community Statement will be of assistance to practitioners. Further details are available at www.dca.gov.uk.

12 CIVIL PARTNERSHIPS

The Civil Partnership Act 2004 received Royal Assent in November 2004 and includes the provisions giving the surviving partner of a same-sex relationship the same rights to succeed to tenancies and to apply to the court for a transfer of a tenancy in the event of a breakdown of the relationship. The Act is not yet in force.

13 COAL AUTHORITY MINING REPORTS

The Coal Authority has introduced insurance cover within all residential property coal-mining reports, for loss in property value that may arise as a consequence of providing certain types of changed mining information. It has also introduced an interpretive report service providing additional value-added analysis and advice where mine entries (shafts and adits) are disclosed in coal-mining reports.

The authority launched the next generation mining reports and surface damage system (MRSDS2) in April 2004, which future-proofs the current service and provides a fully scaleable property search enquiry logging capacity to cope with up to ten million searches per annum.

Following discussion with the Law Society, the Coal Authority's expedited mining report service will now only be available to credit account customers, or where the full fee (including the expedite element) is paid in advance, either by credit or debit card (over the telephone) or by cheque (postal enquiries). These changes have been necessary to help remedy audit reconciliation difficulties between mining report enquiries logged and payment received, and because of the increased cost of debt-collection administration.

On 1 January 2005, the Coal Authority increased its fees for coal-mining reports and related services as follows:

Type of Enquiry	New Fee	Old Fee
Residential property search – postal or telephone service users	£24	£19
Residential property search – Coal Authority online service users	£20	£16
Non-residential property or development site search – all users	£50	£45
No search required certificate (online service users only)	£10	£ 7.50
Subsidence damage claim search (Con29M enquiry nine only)	£10	£10
Claims history search	£58.75	£58.75
Expedited fee (payable additional to the above)	£39	£39
Interpretive report (subsequent to disclosure of mine entry in residential coal-mining report)	£47	£47

14 LAND REGISTRY – ELECTRONIC OFFICIAL COPIES

Land Registry Direct and National Land Information Service customers can request electronic official copies of Land Registry registers of title and title plans and also caution registers and plans, where the Land Registry holds the original in electronic format. Future enhancements will also provide for electronic Land Registry official copies of documents and the electronic delivery of official search certificates and land charges official search certificates. The official copy will be issued in the form of a PDF file. The Land Registry considers that a print from the PDF file will be an official copy, provided it has not been modified or corrupted since receipt. If the PDF file is forwarded, it will (provided it has not been modified or corrupted) constitute an official copy and a print from it will be an official copy. Solicitors who need to satisfy themselves that a document is an official copy should look for two considerations – its appearance and where it came from. Does it look like an official copy and are there any obvious discrepancies, such as no watermark or in the form and order of the information? Did the document purport to come from LRD or NLIS or from a person whose standing is such as to make it likely to be an official copy? Further details and information can be found at www.landregistry.gov.uk.

15 LAND REGISTRY – ELECTRONIC K17 AND K18 LAND CHARGES CERTIFICATES OF RESULT OF SEARCH

Since Monday 27 September 2004, Land Charges certificates of result of search (Forms K17 and K18) are, in the circumstances set out below, issued in electronic format to Land Registry Direct and National Land Information Service customers.

Except as mentioned below, an electronic certificate of result of search is issued by way of a PDF file when a customer has made, via LRD or NLIS, a Form K15 (Application for an official search) or K16 (Application for an official search (Bankruptcy only)) search; and has requested that the certificate of result of search is issued in electronic format (i.e. by way of a PDF file).

The PDF file the customer receives is the certificate of result of search and so a certificate will not be issued in paper form.

An electronic certificate cannot be provided where the names to be searched are either complex names, e.g. Peers of the Realm or unlimited companies or corporations or a local authority. In these circumstances, a paper certificate of result of search will always be issued by post or DX.

Further details and information can be found at www.landregistry.gov.uk.

16 LAND REGISTRY – ELECTRONIC REQUISITIONS

The Land Registry has introduced e-mail to send requests for information arising during a title registration. The Registry will automatically send requisitions by e-mail where an e-mail address is provided on the application form. However, it will not look for an e-mail address on any other documentation, and conveyancers who want to receive information requests by post should not provide an e-mail address on the form.

17 LAND REGISTRY – CHANGE OF POLICY

On 1 October 2004, the Land Registry discontinued its arrangement with mortgage lenders under which the original charge bearing a specified MD reference is automatically retained or issued following completion of its registration. From that date, the provisions of rule 203 of the Land Registration Rules 2003 applies to all applications to register a charge. This provides that a request may be made to return all or any of the documents accompanying an application. No formal request is required as it is presumed that the original deed or document is to be returned where it is accompanied by a certified copy. A conveyancer must ascertain from a lender whether it requires the Land Registry to retain the original charge or not. If it does then no copy should be supplied. If it does not then a certified copy should accompany the application.

18   THE BARKER REPORT

Following the 2003 Budget, Kate Barker (a member of the Monetary Policy Committee) was asked to review issues affecting housing supply in the UK. Her report was published in 2004 and it concluded that the number of houses being built is not keeping pace with demand. The Report makes 36 recommendations which, if implemented, will have a significant impact on the planning system.

The Report recommends that a revised Planning Policy Guidance Note 3 should ensure transparency and consistency in approach in calculating regional housing requirements. A single body in each region should be responsible for setting its own target to improve market affordability. It suggests that PPG 3 should have regard to competition in the allocation of sites.

The Report recommends that local plans should be more realistic in allocating land for housing. Land should be allocated to cover previous historic shortfalls and an additional 20-40% should be included to provide a headroom to respond to signals of market 'disequilibrium', such as worsening market affordability and rising numbers of housing transactions.

The Report recommends that English Partnerships should have a lead role in delivering complex sites, through master planning, remediating contaminated land and developing supporting infrastructure. It also recommends that greater use should be made of Urban Development Corporations and New Towns. The Report recommends that planning authority resources should be strengthened; by increasing the range of permitted development rights, implementation of the proposed Local Development Orders, and increasing planning fees.

There should be two additional routes to obtain planning permission:

a) an outline only route, which would contain more detail than is currently required, but after which all reserved matters would be dealt with by planning officers; and

b) a 'design code route' which would result in the granting of a Local Development Order to cover the identified site and remove the need for any subsequent planning permission, provided the code requirements were met.

It also suggests that, where planning officers and house builders disagree on specific design issues, the difference should be dealt with by arbitration, possibly through the Commission for Architecture and the Built Environment. The Report suggests that planning authorities should agree build out rates for large sites.

The Report recommends that infrastructure providers, such as the water companies and the Highways Agency, should be involved at an early stage in developing the regional strategy, and that their powers of objection to a development should only be allowed to block the grant of planning permission if the benefits of the new development are clearly outweighed by the infrastructure costs. Ofgem and Ofwat should develop guidance on establishing a fair price for developer charges for extensions or alterations to infrastructure.

Most controversially, the Report recommends that section 106 should be scaled back to deal with direct impact mitigation and that the Government should use tax measures to extract some of the windfall gain that accrues to landowners from the sale of land for residential development. It suggests that the tax rate should be such as to cover at least the estimated local authority gain from section 106 contributions and provide additional resources to boost housing supply. Granting planning permission would be contingent on payment of the tax which may vary between brownfield and greenfield land and in other circumstances. A proportion of the revenue generated would be given directly to local authorities. The basis of the tax calculation would be actual increase in values and/or using the existing twice-yearly land valuations undertaken by the Valuation Office.

19   *LAND REGISTRY PUBLICATIONS*

The Land Registry has published the following:

Practice Guide 11 – Inspection and applications for official copies (1/12/2004);

Practice Guide 12 – Official searches and outline applications (14/6/2004);

Practice Guide 19 – Notices, restrictions and the protection of third party interests in the register (1/12/2004);

Practice Guide 24 – Private trusts of land (31/12/2004);

Practice Guide 29 – Registration of legal charges and deeds of variation of charge (18/10/2004);

Practice Guide 43 – Applications in connection with court proceedings, insolvency and tax liability (1/12/2004);

Practice Guide 48 – Implied covenants (1/12/2004);

Practice Guide 49 – Rejection of applications for registration (1/2/2005);

Practice Guide 51 – Areas served by Land Registry Offices (14/2/2005);

Practice Guide 52 – Easements claimed by prescription and statutory rights of way for vehicles (1/7/2004);

Practice Guide 57 – Exempting documents from the general right to inspect and copy (1/12/2004);

Practice Guide 59 – Receiving and replying to requisitions by email (12/8/2004);

Practice Guide 60 – Commonhold (1/9/2004);

Practice Guide 61 – Telephone Services (credit account holders only) (1/7/2004);

Public Guide 1 – A guide to the information we keep and how you can obtain it (31/12/2004);

Public Guide 13 – Applications for first registration made by the owner in person (1/12/2004);

Public Guide 15 – Your rights under the Freedom of Information Act 2000 (1/12/2004).

Further details and information can be found at www.landregistry.gov.uk.

20 LAND REGISTRY – APPLICATIONS SENT TO THE WRONG LAND REGISTRY OFFICE

With effect from 14 February 2005, the Land Registry will return to the applicant any application that is not lodged at the proper office. This may result in loss of priority. The requirement to lodge applications at the proper office is covered by the Land Registration Act 2002 and 2003 Rules. Rule 15(3) states that an application is received when it is delivered:

a) to the designated proper office in accordance with an order under section 100(3) of the Act; or

b) to the registrar in accordance with a written agreement as to delivery made between the registrar and the applicant or between the registrar and the applicant's conveyancer; or

c) to the registrar under the provisions of any relevant notice given under Schedule 2.

Details of the areas covered by each Land Registry office can be found in Practice Guide 51 – Areas served by Land Registry Offices.

21 SDLT – NIL RATE BAND DISCRETIONARY TRUST

The Inland Revenue has issued guidance on SDLT in relation to Nil Rate Band discretionary trusts. The guidance confirms that the transfer of an interest in land to a beneficiary is a land transaction for SDLT purposes. If the transferor gives consideration, SDLT is payable (subject to value). The guidance outlines the SDLT treatment of common examples of Nil Rate Band transactions, including a straightforward charge or an IOU from the surviving spouse (which is taxable). Further details and information can be found at www.inlandrevenue.gov.uk/so/nilband.htm.

22 INHERITANCE TAX MANUAL

IR Capital Taxes have announced that a new guidance manual, the *Inheritance Tax Manual*, will be published. It will incorporate guidance previously given in the Advanced Instruction, General Examination and Debt Management Manuals, all of which have now been withdrawn. The new manual will also incorporate the text of the Inheritance Tax Double Taxation Conventions and Agreements. Further details and information can be found at www.inlandrevenue.gov.uk/manuals/ctmmanual/index.htm.

23 CGT – ALLOWABLE EXPENDITURE: EXPENSES INCURRED BY PERSONAL REPRESENTATIVES AND CORPORATE TRUSTEES

A new Statement of Practice, SP2/04, has replaced SP8/94 in relation to certain expenses incurred by the personal representatives of deceased persons where the death in question occurred on or after 6 April 2004, and to expenses incurred by corporate trustees in making transfers and disposals on or after 6 April 2004.

The new Statements of Practice sets out standard scales of allowable expenses which may be used for certain purposes of the Taxation of Chargeable Gains Act 1992 in place of the actual allowable expenditure incurred.

The main changes introduced by SP2/04 are an increase in the monetary values set out in the scales, broadly in line with the increase in the Retail Price Index since 1994, and the introduction of two new higher bands (over £1,000,000 and over £5,000,000) to cover larger estates.

24 NATIONAL CONVEYANCING PROTOCOL

The fifth edition of the National Conveyancing Protocol came into effect on 30 November 2004.

The TransAction forms have also been revised and the current editions are:

Seller's Property Information Form (Fourth Edition);

Seller's Leasehold Information Form (Third Edition);

Fixtures, Fittings and Contents Form (Fourth Edition);

Completion Information and Requisitions on Title (Second Edition).

In addition, a new form, the Seller's Commonhold Information Form (First Edition), is due to be published in 2005.

25 *ACCOUNTING FOR LEASEHOLDERS' MONIES AND SUMMARIES OF TENANTS' RIGHTS AND OBLIGATIONS*

A consultation paper was issued by the Office of the Deputy Prime Minister on 25 June 2004 seeking views on the provisions in the Commonhold and Leasehold Reform Act 2002 that make changes to the way in which service charge monies are held, and the information that is provided to service charge payers. It is concerned with service charge trust funds under section 42 of the Landlord and Tenant Act 1985. In future it will be necessary for monies in respect of each block of flats to be held in separate funds, each to be called a 'section 42A account'. The consultation period ended on 24 September 2004.

26 *SDLT – PARTNERSHIPS*

The transfer of an interest in land into a partnership, the acquisition of an interest in a partnership (where the partnership property includes an interest in land) and the transfer of an interest in land out of a partnership, were originally excluded from Stamp Duty Land Tax. Draft legislation was published on 20 October 2003 and, following consultation, these transactions were brought within the scope of Stamp Duty Land Tax by the Finance Act 2004.

As a result, Stamp Duty Land Tax is now charged on the following transactions:

● Where an interest in land is transferred into a partnership, either by an existing partner or by a person in exchange for an interest in that partnership. Stamp Duty Land Tax will be chargeable, at the appropriate rate, on a proportion of the market value of that land interest. The proportion will be equal to the proportion of the land interest transferred to the other partners as measured by their partnership.

● Where partnership property includes an interest in land and arrangements are in place so that either an existing partner transfers all or part of their partnership interest, to a person who is or becomes a partner, for money or money's worth; or a person becomes a partner and an existing partner reduces their partnership share (or ceases to be a partner) and withdraws money or money's worth from the partnership, then Stamp Duty Land Tax will be chargeable, at the appropriate rate, on the person acquiring the interest or increased interest, on a proportion of the market value of the land interest so transferred. The proportion will be equal to the increased (or new) partnership share held by the acquiring partner. Where a partnership transfers an interest in land to a partner or former partner, Stamp Duty Land Tax will be chargeable, at the appropriate rate, on the person acquiring the interest, on the proportion of the market value of the land interest transferred on which tax (which includes *ad valorem* stamp duty or, for transactions executed before 20 October 2003, fixed duty) has not previously been paid.

27 INSOLVENCY REFORMS

On 1 April 2004, the Enterprise Act 2002 introduced reforms to the Insolvency Act 1986 which affect the way in which trustees in bankruptcy handle a bankrupt's matrimonial home or other jointly owned property. Section 261 of the 2002 Act has inserted a new section 283A into the Insolvency Act 1986. This provision forces trustees to deal with any interest held by the bankrupt in a home that, at the date of the bankruptcy, was either the sole or principal residence of the bankrupt, or of the bankrupt's spouse, or of a former spouse of the bankrupt within a period of three years beginning with the date of the bankruptcy.

In order to comply with this three-year rule, a trustee in bankruptcy must have taken one or more of the following steps:

- Realised its interest.

- Applied for an order for sale in respect of the property.

- Applied for an order for possession of the property.

- Applied for a charge under section 313 of the Insolvency Act 1986.

- The trustee and the bankrupt must agree that the latter will incur a specified liability to its estate (with or without interest), in consideration of which the trustee's interest will no longer form part of the estate.

As a result of these reforms, a trustee in bankruptcy must now bear in mind that it now has only three years in which to realise any interest it may have in property comprised in the bankrupt's estate, and that it will lose the ability to claim an interest in property following an unsuccessful application to the court to secure or release an interest in property.

28 *LAND REGISTRY – DEFINING THE SERVICE E-CONVEYANCING*

On 21 July 2004, the Land Registry published 'Land Registry – Defining the service e-conveyancing'. The purpose of this document is to provide an early yet definitive statement of the services that are needed to realise the E-Conveyancing vision as set out in *The Strategy for the Implementation of E-Conveyancing in England and Wales*. This definitive statement is needed to enable all stakeholders in the conveyancing process to have a common understanding of how E-Conveyancing will work in practice.

The document describes the component services of E-Conveyancing; how they will relate to each other and the functions they will be required to have. It has five parts:

- Part 1 describes the E-Conveyancing three service model.

- Part 2 describes the specific functions of the Central E-Conveyancing Service.

- Part 3 describes the specific functions of the electronic funds transfer service.

- Part 4 introduces Land Registry's thinking on channel services.

- Part 5 describes the overarching functions required of the entire E-Conveyancing service.

29 *SOLICITORS PRACTICE RULES 1990*

Practice rules 6(3) (solicitor acting for lender and borrower) and 6A (seller's solicitor dealing with more than one prospective buyer) were amended on 9 February 2005 by the Solicitors Practice (Conveyancing) Amendment Rule 2005.

A new paragraph (c)(ixA) has been inserted into rule 6(3) to allow a solicitor to accept appropriate instructions from a lender when acting in the purchase and mortgage of commonhold property. A new paragraph (2)(ivA) has been inserted into the approved certificate of title, set out in the appendix to rule 6(3), to cover commonhold property.

Additional amendments have been made to paragraphs (c)(ii) and (d) of the approved certificate of title, to reflect the new Stamp Duty Land Tax regime and the abolition of charge certificates.

Rule 6A has been amended to clarify that it applies to commonhold transactions.

30 SDLT PRACTITIONERS' NEWSLETTERS

The Inland Revenue publishes a regular newsletter on Stamp Duty Land Tax for practitioners. Copies are available at www.inlandrevenue.gov.uk/so/bull_news_flyers_sdlt.htm.

Details of the published newsletters are as follows:

Issue 1 – Common errors on completing SDLT 1 returns.

Issue 2 – Includes information on Penalties for late land transaction returns, reminders on completion of the SDLT 1 and common queries regarding leases.

Issue 3 – Includes information on SDLT 1 – errors and processing issues, SDLT CD-ROM, SDLT 8s: when they will be issued, Multiple Acquisitions, Advice on when you can use an SDLT 60 instead of an SDLT1 to notify a transaction, Complaints and Supplementary forms: sending photocopies.

Issue 4 – Includes information on the SDLT Pilot, Relief claimed on 'Right to Buy' transactions, one cheque submitted covering multiple applications, leases and SDLT and 'nil-rate band discretionary trusts'.

Issue 5 – Special issue on the SDLT CD-ROM.

Issue 6 – Includes information on SDLT 6 guidance, which aspects of SDLT present the most difficulties, the new version of SDLT 4, and reversionary leases.

31 LANDS TRIBUNAL – PRACTICE DIRECTION

The Lands Tribunal has revised its Practice Direction in the light of a number of changes, including section 175 of the Commonhold and Leasehold Reform Act 2002 on permission to appeal and costs. It also restates, in slightly modified form, the approach to the grant of permission and the way in which appeals are to be dealt with. Section 6 is new and makes clear the Tribunal's practice in ordering statements of case and replies in references. There is a requirement in paragraph 14.13, following the Court of Appeal in *Railtrack plc v Guinness Ltd* ([2003] EWCA Civ 188), that experts relying on computer-based valuations must agree to employ a common model that can be made available to the Tribunal. Section 20 on costs has been modified and clarified, distinguishing more clearly between particular jurisdictions. It reflects the Court of Appeal decision in *Purfleet Farms Ltd v Secretary of State for the Environment* ([2002] RVR 368) on the approach in compulsory purchase compensation cases. In restrictive covenant cases the approach is that set out in *Re Fairclough Homes Ltd's Application* (LP/30/2001) and other recent cases. The revised Practice Direction came into force on 4 January 2005 and is available at www.landstribunal.gov.uk/practiceproc/lands_practice.htm.

32 LICENSING

The Licensing Act 2003 received Royal Assent on 10 July 2003 and follows on from the white paper, published in April 2000, which looked at reforming alcohol and entertainment licensing (*Time for Reform: Proposals for the Modernisation of our Licensing Laws*, CM4696). The purpose of the Act is to promote the four fundamental licensing objectives, which are:

1. The prevention of crime and disorder.

2. The promotion of public safety.

3. The prevention of public nuisance.

4. The protection of children from harm.

The Act unifies the various different licensing systems into a single integrated scheme licensing the sale of alcohol, the provision of public entertainment and late night refreshments.

The licensing authorises the provision of 'licensable activities' through a system of:

● Personal licences.

● Premises licences.

● Club premises certificates.

● Temporary event notices.

The Secretary of State's guidance under section 182 was issued on 7 July 2004. At this time, licensing authorities began preparing their new licensing policy statements. The 'First Appointed Day' from which licences can be applied for under the new system was 7 February 2005. The 'Second Appointed Day', which is the day when the new system will come fully into force, will be ten months after the First Appointed Day.

a) Personal licences

These authorise individuals to sell or supply alcohol or authorise the sale or supply of alcohol for consumption on or off premises. To qualify for a personal licence an individual must:

i)   be 18 or over;

ii) possess an accredited licensing qualification which will ensure that the licensee knows the law but is also aware of the broader social responsibility that comes with the sale of alcohol; and

iii) have a clean criminal record (subject to some exceptions).

Personal licences last for ten years and are renewable unless they are suspended, surrendered or forfeit by the court. Under so-called 'grandfather' provisions, most people currently holding a Justice's Licence can convert the existing alcohol licence into a new personal licence.

b) Premises licences

A premises licence will authorise the holder of the licence to use the premises for 'licensable activities'. A licence can be held by an individual or by a corporate entity and the licence details the licensable activities to be undertaken at the premises. An operating plan or schedule is a new feature of the Licensing Act and is central to the application for a premises licence. It consists of a description of the style and character of the business to be run from the premises and should include:

i) details of the times during which the licensable activities are to take place;

ii) if open at any other times, when the premises are open;

iii) if the licence is required only for a limited period, what that period is;

iv) where the licensable activities include the supply of alcohol, the details of the designated premises supervisor; and

v) steps which the applicant proposes to take to promote the licensing objectives.

The premises licence will incorporate operating conditions fixed on the basis of the operators requirements and residents' views, as well as police and Fire Authority assessments. These licences are transferable and may also be varied on application.

c) Designated premises supervisor

The sale of alcohol is considered to have greater responsibility than other regulated entertainment and that is why a personal licence is required by individuals who supply or sell alcohol. The 'Designated Premises Supervisor' is required to ensure that there is always one specified individual, among probably a number of personal licence holders working in a premises, identified as having the day-to-day responsibility for running the premises. It is considered essential that the Police, Fire Officers or the Licensing Authority can immediately identify the designated premises supervisor as their point of contact. The designated premises supervisor is to be specified on the premises licence and, if he changes, the new designated premises supervisor is to be notified to the Licensing Authority.

d) Local authorities as licensing authorities

Previously, the responsibility for granting and monitoring the various licences was divided amongst different authorities; for instance, local authorities dealt with cinema licences, whereas the local licensing justices dealt with alcohol licences. Under the Licensing Act, the new Licensing Authority is the Local Authority. The Licensing Authority has to promote the four licensing objectives of the legislation and, in carrying out its licensing functions, has to have regard to the guidance issued by the Secretary of State under section 182 of the Licensing Act 2003. Every three years the licensing authority must publish its own policy with respect to exercising its licensing functions after consultation with the local police, the Fire Authority and other relevant local bodies.

e) Other provisions

Flexible opening hours is a key feature. The Licensing Act brings with it the potential for up to 24-hour, seven days a week opening in order to minimise the social disorder and binge-drinking associated with the current regimented 11pm closing time. There is detailed guidance on permitted opening hours which, ultimately, will be subject to consideration of the impact on local residents. Fees are to be set centrally with no local authority discretion to vary them.

There will be a new system of temporary permitted activities which allow extensions for premises licences and the sale of alcohol by non-licence holders within permitted limits after a straightforward notification process. This will allow specific events to be held, such as a wedding reception, parties for sporting events, e.g. World Cup final, etc.

Boats undertaking 'licensable activities' will require a premises licence, as will wholesalers, when selling to the public.

The sanctions available to local authorities are much more wide-ranging and flexible and include the suspension and forfeiture of licences.

f) Transitional phase

Although conversion from an old licence to a new one is not automatic, if an application is made, the existing licence will generally be converted into a licence under the new scheme; however, it will include all the restrictions and limitation of the old licence. If licensees wish to take advantage of the more flexible range of opening hours or to diversify their business, they will need to make an application for a variation of the existing licence. As an applicant will, in any event, have to do the work by producing an operating schedule as part of the application for the premises licence, it would be prudent to make any application for variation at the same time as the initial application to convert the licence rather than waiting for the new system to come into force.

33 PLANNING POLICY GUIDANCE 3: HOUSING

PPG 3 was updated on 24 January 2005. Paragraph 18 now states that Regional Spatial Strategies should set out how planning at the local level should assist in meeting identified rural housing needs, including the needs of gypsies and travellers. Local authorities should make land available within or adjoining rural communities to enable local requirements to be met, and should promote rural exception policies, solely for affordable housing on land which would not be released for general housing. The affordable housing should be secured to remain as such. Paragraph 42(a) requires planning authorities to look favourably on housing applications on land identified for mixed use as industrial/commercial use, where those uses are no longer required.

34 *HM LAND REGISTRY – E-LODGEMENT PILOT*

The Land Registry has started an E-Lodgement Pilot. In February 2002 the Land Registry launched its first E-Lodgement Service. Delivered using Land Registry Direct, customers were able to apply online at the touch of a button for simple changes of the register to be made (such as changing the name of a registered proprietor on marriage or divorce). However, the system was very limited, only enabling five types of no-fee applications to be lodged online. This latest E-Lodgement Project is looking to go beyond the limited functionality of the initial service and will introduce, over three distinct phases, a system that allows all application forms to be submitted to Land Registry electronically. The types of applications that can be lodged by each phase are set out below:

Phase One

- Forms with no fee or a fixed fee.

- No attachments.

- No electronic signature required.

- No automatic update to the register.

- Internal system to process applications.

Phase Two

- Forms with variable fee.

- Forms with attachments.

- Forms requiring electronic signatures.

Phase Three

● Forms requiring Stamp Duty Land Tax.

The Phase One pilot scheme started on 14 February 2005. and enabled the following forms to be lodged electronically.

Non fee paying forms:

MH forms.

MH1: registration of notice of matrimonial home rights.

MH2: renewal of registration of matrimonial home rights.

MH4: cancellation of matrimonial home rights notice.

UN forms.

UN2: removal of unilateral notice.

UN4: cancellation of unilateral notice.

WCT: withdrawal of a caution.

RX4: withdrawal of a restriction.

CCD: cancellation of a caution against dealings.

Plus the existing five applications types in Land Registry Direct.

Fee paying forms:

RX1: enter a restriction.

RX2: order to disapply or modify a restriction.

UN1: enter a unilateral notice.

ADV2: register a person to be notified of an application for adverse possession.

UT1: upgrading of a title.

(Forms MH1, MH2, MH4 and RX1 were lodged electronically from the launch of the pilot on 14 February 2005, the other forms listed were due to be launched on 21 March 2005.)

The pilot will run for three months, initially with selected users lodging applications through Land Registry Direct. However, during this pilot period other methods of delivery will also be explored, including NLIS and Case Management Systems. Dates for Phase Two and Three of the E-Lodgement Project have yet to be agreed and are subject to legislative requirements.

35 PERSONAL SEARCHES: GUIDANCE FOR LOCAL AUTHORITIES AND PERSONAL SEARCHERS

The ODPM has issued guidance intended to promote good practice and working relations between local authority staff and personal searchers of the Local Land Charges Register (and other local authority records open to public inspection). The guidance is available at www.odpm.gov.uk/stellent/groups/odpm_housing/ documents/page/odpm_house_035679.pdf.

Part D

THE WAY FORWARD

1 *PLANNING OBLIGATIONS*

The Government has published a revised draft circular on planning obligations, which sets out some possible changes to the current system to be made in advance of major reforms which are likely to take place during the course of the next two to three years in response to the recommendations of the final report of the Barker Review of Housing Supply. The document can be found at www.odpm.gov.uk and the consultation period ended on 25 January 2005.

2 *CONSULTATION PAPER ON MINERALS POLICY STATEMENT 1: PLANNING AND MINERALS*

The Government has published a consultation paper seeking comments on a draft of a new Minerals Policy Statement (MPS) 1: *Planning and Minerals* and its associated Good Practice Guidance (GPG). MPS 1 will replace Minerals Planning Guidance note 1: *General Considerations and the Development Plan System* (MPG 1). The document can be found at www.odpm.gov.uk and the consultation period ended on 28 February 2005.

3 *FURTHER PROPOSED CHANGES TO THE SYSTEM OF PLANNING FEES IN ENGLAND*

The Government has published a consultation paper putting forward for consultation further proposals for changes to the system of planning fees for 2005/6, to be introduced on 1 April 2005. The document can be found at www.odpm.gov.uk and the consultation period ended on 28 January 2005.

4 TEMPORARY STOP NOTICES

The Office of the Deputy Prime Minister has published draft Temporary Stop Notice Regulations, and an associated draft Circular for consultation. The temporary stop notice provisions in Part 4 of the Planning and Compulsory Purchase Act 2004 inserted sections 171E to 171H to the Town and Country Planning Act 1990. The Act gives local planning authorities a new discretionary enforcement power to be able to issue a temporary stop notice at the start of unauthorised development, before an enforcement notice is served, thus speeding up the process of enforcement. The decision to use the 'temporary stop notice' will be at the discretion of local planning authorities, if they think that there has been a breach of planning control and they consider that it is expedient that the activity is stopped immediately. The draft regulations restrict the use of temporary stop notices in certain circumstances and specify activity not prohibited by a temporary stop notice. The draft Circular gives guidance on the temporary stop notice provisions in the Act. The document can be found at www.odpm.gov.uk and the consultation period ended on 26 January 2005.

5 CHANGES TO THE DEVELOPMENT CONTROL SYSTEM

In October 2003, a consultation document was published giving some details of the Government's planning reform agenda. The document contained suggested amendments to the Town and Country Planning (General Development Procedure) Order 1995 (GDPO) and additional guidance relating to provisions contained in the Planning and Compulsory Purchase Bill – now the Planning and Compulsory Purchase Act 2004. As a result of discussions in Parliament during the passage of the Bill and the consultation exercise, a number of changes have been made and the government decided to re-consult on the revised proposals. The document can be found at www.odpm.gov.uk and the consultation period ended on 22 February 2005.

6 PLANNING FOR GYPSY AND TRAVELLER SITES

During the passage of the Planning and Compulsory Purchase Act through Parliament, the Government made a commitment to review the guidance contained within DoE Circular 1/94 'Gypsy Sites and Planning' as part of the ODPM's ongoing review of Gypsies and Travellers Policy. The advice in the Circular covers the procedures to be followed in ensuring that the planning system recognises, protects and facilitates the traditional lifestyle of gypsies and travellers by identifying and making provision in developments plans for their land and accommodation requirements. The key changes are:

- A change to the definition of 'gypsy'. The new definition recognises that gypsies may stop travelling, either permanently or temporarily, for health or educational reasons or because of caring responsibilities.

- A requirement that local authorities identify suitable sites for gypsies and travellers in their development plan documents. Only exceptionally will it be acceptable to meet needs by specifying criteria for the identification of sites without identifying any specific sites.

- Improved guidance on drafting the criteria in development plans against which applications for sites not allocated in the plan will be judged. The existing Circular said that criteria should be clear and realistic, and the new guidance strengthens this advice saying they should be fair, reasonable, realistic and effective in delivering sites.

- An explanation of how local housing assessments will assist local authorities to quantify the level of need and how the new planning system and the involvement of Regional Housing Boards will translate that need into allocations in the planning process.

- A section on local authorities' responsibilities under the Race Relations Act.

- The inclusion of advice on how local authorities should seek to engage with gypsies and travellers and build trust.

The document can be found at www.odpm.gov.uk and the consultation period ended on 18 March 2005.

7 CONSULTATION ON PLANNING POLICY STATEMENT 10: PLANNING FOR SUSTAINABLE WASTE MANAGEMENT

This consultation sought views and comments on the draft of the new Planning Policy Statement (PPS) 10 Planning for Sustainable Waste Management. The intention is that PPS 10, together with an accompanying practice guide should, in due course, replace Planning Policy Guidance Note 10 (PPG 10) Planning and Waste Management, published in 1999. The document can be found at www.odpm.gov.uk and the consultation period ended on 11 March 2005.

8 PLANNING POLICY STATEMENT 9: BIODIVERSITY AND GEOLOGICAL CONSERVATION

This consultation paper sought comments on a draft of a new Planning Policy Statement (PPS) on Biodiversity and Geological Conservation. The intention is that this PPS, together with a new Government Circular (which will cover relevant legislative provisions) and good practice guidance should, in due course, replace Planning Policy Guidance Note 9 (PPG 9), *Nature Conservation* (published in October 1994). The document can be found at www.odpm.gov.uk and the consultation period ended on 9 December 2004.

189

9   *EXECUTION OF DEEDS*

The Government has laid a draft regulatory reform order before Parliament, the Regulatory Reform (Execution of Deeds and Documents) Order 2004, which will eradicate inconsistencies between a number of different legislative provisions that govern the way in which companies execute deeds. The Order will enable companies who still affix seals to documents to dispense with the signature of the company secretary and to replace it with the signature of another director instead, and will also make welcome changes to the presumptions of due execution and delivery which apply for the benefit of purchasers.

10   *GAMBLING BILL*

The Gambling Bill was introduced in the House of Commons on 18 October 2004 and published on 19 October. The most controversial parts of the Bill relate to casinos. Casinos will be classed in three size categories: small, large, and regional. The class into which a casino falls will be dependent on, among other things, its floor area. Only regional casinos, which must be at least 5,000m^2 in size, will be allowed to install machines that pay out unlimited prizes. Other casinos, bingo halls, licensed betting premises and premises licensed as adult gaming centres will be allowed to install machines that pay out prizes capped at amounts fixed by the Government.

Large and regional casinos will also be allowed to hold bingo games, which will increase competition for many existing bingo halls.

Premises licensed as family entertainment centres, to which children have access, will be allowed only the lower categories of gaming machines, and the Bill offers much less scope for premises without a gaming licence (such as fish and chip shops, pubs, amusement arcades and members' clubs) to offer gaming machines.

11 REGISTRATION OF SECURITY INTERESTS: COMPANY CHARGES AND PROPERTY OTHER THAN LAND

The Law Commission has published a consultation paper reviewing the law that governs the registration of charges that companies may grant over their assets as security for loans, and more generally the law of security over property other than land. At present, charges created by companies must be registered at Companies House within 21 days. Charges over registered land must then be separately registered at the Land Registry. The consultation paper suggests a whole new legislative scheme, which would introduce:

- A wholly electronic filing system, under which the 21-day limit for registration will no longer apply.

- The validity and priority of charges over land will not be dependent on registration at Companies House and registration with the Land Registry will suffice.

The consultation paper can be found at www.lawcom.gov.uk and the consultation period ended on 2 October 2004.

12 CAPITAL AND INCOME IN TRUSTS: CLASSIFICATION AND APPORTIONMENT

The Law Commission has published a consultation paper which sets out the current law on apportionment and outlines previous proposals for reform in England and Wales and in Scotland. Apportionment covers whether something received by a trustee is to be treated as capital or income, and how should trustees split between beneficiaries – on the basis of capital or income? The paper makes proposals for a new scheme for the classification and apportionment of trust receipts and expenses and invites the views of interested parties on these proposals. The consultation paper can be found at www.lawcom.gov.uk and the consultation period ended on 31 October 2004.

13 LAND REGISTRY CONSULTATION PAPER ON PRESCRIBED FORMS OF LEASES

The Land Registry has published a consultation paper on standardised lease information to make it easier to for it to understand the principal terms of the leases that are submitted to it and to streamline its registration procedures. The paper sets out two alternative methods of presenting prescribed information. The first is the introduction of Form L1 (which resembles the existing transfer forms), which would form the introduction to, and a prescribed part of, each registrable lease. The other is the use of some prescribed clauses in registrable leases, which would need to be included at the beginning of each registrable lease. The consultation paper can be found at www.landregistry.gov.uk/consultations and the consultation period ended on 10 December 2004.

14 COMMERCIAL LEASE REFORM

In February 2005, the Office of the Deputy Prime Minister published the final report compiled by Reading University, entitled *Monitoring the 2002 Code of Practice for Commercial Leases*. This followed the publication in April 2004 of an interim report. The final report is available at www.odpm.gov.uk/stellent/groups/odpm_urbanpolicy/documents/page/odpm_urbpol_035504.pdf, whilst the interim report is available at www.odpm.gov.uk/stellent/groups/odpm_urbanpolicy/documents/page/odpm_urbpol_028392.pdf.

The overall aim of the research project was to assess the impact of the Code on the commercial leasing market, so that the Government can decide whether to introduce statutory controls to replace the Code.

The report provides an independent view about:

a) whether lease structures are becoming more flexible;

b) the extent to which tenants are being offered a choice of alternative terms;

c) the extent to which the Code is influencing the market; and

d) the extent to which small business tenants are aware of the Code.

The report shows that upwards-only rent reviews are still 'almost universal', but concludes that 'the picture is one of improving flexibility: reduced lease lengths, more tenant breaks' and 'more leases without any rent review'. The Report highlights that the Code has had a greater impact than its predecessor in that it has been more widely disseminated, but that it is having very little direct impact on individual lease negotiations.

15 *UPWARDS-ONLY RENT REVIEWS*

In May 2004, the Government published its consultation paper *Commercial property leases: options for deterring or outlawing the use of upward only rent review clauses.* The consultation paper can be found at www.odpm.gov.uk and the consultation period ended on 30 September 2004.

The background to this consultation is that the Government believes that inflexible leases are bad for the economy, and is committed to promoting more choice and flexibility in the commercial property leasing market. It is concerned that tenants sometimes have little choice over the terms they are offered, and believes that upward-only rent reviews result in property risks falling disproportionately on tenants, leaving them exposed during downturns in the market.

The Government was disappointed by the findings set out in the interim report from Reading University, *Monitoring the 2002 Code of Practice for Commercial Leases*, which suggests that the Code has had very little impact on commercial leases. It therefore decided to consult on options to deter or prohibit the use of upward-only rent review clauses so that it can legislate at the earliest opportunity, if it decides that legislation is appropriate.

The Government has indicated that it will use the final report on the Commercial Lease Code, and the responses to the consultation, to inform its decision. It wants to know why upward-only rent review clauses have continued to be prevalent in a low-inflation business environment, which is very different from the high-inflation environment in which they were first developed, and has asked for comments on several different legislative options.

The consultation paper sets out six different options. It does not make any recommendations at this stage, but simply invites comments on whether the Government should intervene to prohibit or deter the use of upward-only rent review clauses, and on the merits of each of these options. It also asks whether there are any other viable alternatives to statutory intervention, bearing in mind the impact of the two successive voluntary Codes of Practice, and seeks views on what effect these options would have on inflexibility and lack of choice in the commercial property leasing market; what impact these options would have on the market, on rents, on development and funding, and on largescale investments and those of marginal economic viability, and which of the options would be preferable.

The different legislative options set out in the paper are as follows:

Option 1: Do nothing
The Government could choose not to legislate and would simply continue to press the property industry to adhere to the Commercial Lease Code. However, the Government is concerned that inaction would do nothing to eradicate inflexible leasing practices, and the paper seems to suggest that the Government does not think that this is a viable option.

Option 2: Ban upward-only rent review clauses

The Government would enact primary legislation requiring any periodic rent review to open market rent to be on an upwards or downwards basis. This would mean that reviewed rents would be capped by reference to the open market rent. The legislation would also override any lease provisions permitting only the landlord to initiate reviews, but would not preclude the use of indexation or fixed rental increases that are agreed at the very outset of a lease. The consultation paper acknowledges that it would not be appropriate to legislate to change leases that are already in place, so there would be a two-tier market. The Government would also need to consider whether to direct the courts to impose upward/downward rent reviews in leases that are renewed under Part II of the Landlord and Tenant Act 1954.

Option 3: Ban upward-only rent reviews subject to a floor of the initial rent

The Government could legislate to impose upward/downward reviews, but landlords would be allowed to prohibit rents from falling below the initial rents reserved by their leases, i.e. rent reviews would be capped, but could be made subject to a collar too. There are concerns that such legislation would have no impact at all on shorter leases, where there is only one rent review during the term, and it is recognised that it would not completely eliminate 'overrenting'. Defining the initial rent might be difficult too, if landlords offer rent-free periods, stepped rents or other inducements which could affect the headline rent.

Option 4: Give tenants the right to break if an upward-only review results in a rent that exceeds the open market rent

The Government could enact legislation giving tenants a statutory right to break their leases if an upward-only rent review results in a rent that exceeds the open market rent. The legislation would, in effect, provide tenants with a statutory 'escape route'. The legislation would override any lease provisions permitting only landlords to initiate reviews, to make sure that leases do not prevent tenants from exercising their statutory rights to terminate because they are unable to initiate reviews.

However, the consultation paper acknowledges that there may be several difficulties with this option. Tenants who have in the past tried to operate break clauses that are linked to rent review clauses have not always found it easy to do so, and legislation could trigger litigation between landlords and tenants over the validity of break notices. Ultimately, tenants would have to choose between either paying rents that are higher than the open market rent, which would not eliminate overrenting; or moving to, and fitting out, cheaper premises in a suitable alternative location (which may be hard to find), unless their landlord is willing to reduce the rent to persuade the tenant to stay.

Option 5: Limit lease lengths

The Government could impose a statutory ceiling on lease lengths to neutralise upward-only rent reviews or to limit the period of any over-renting after an upward-only rent review. The comments in the consultation paper, however, suggest that the Government does not consider this a viable option. The consultation paper acknowledges that this would sit uneasily alongside security of tenure, and it is accepted that this would represent a radical intervention in the workings of the property market. It is also acknowledged that tenants who invest considerable sums in their properties will want longer leases. Curtailing lease lengths would add to transaction costs and would not achieve the Government's aim of promoting greater choice and flexibility in commercial leases.

Option 6: Require landlords to give prospective tenants priced options

The Government could legislate to require landlords to offer tenants alternatives to upward-only rent reviews, without prohibiting landlords and tenants from agreeing to use them. The Government would not determine prices, but landlords would be required to offer risk-adjusted pricing on an appropriate basis, using a standard format. The consultation paper accepts that this would achieve the Government's policy aim of promoting greater choice, but says that there would be practical and legal difficulties with this option. It would be very difficult to police and enforce, and it would be difficult to prevent landlords from pricing alternatives to upward-only rent reviews at a level that would be unattractive to tenants. Small business tenants who do not take professional advice would be particularly disadvantaged and could find it difficult to mount an effective legal challenge.

16 USE OF MECHANICALLY PROPELLED VEHICLES ON PUBLIC RIGHTS OF WAY

The Government announced on 20 January 2005 that inappropriate use of public rights of way by mechanically propelled vehicles will be curtailed via legislation. This followed a Defra consultation on proposals to address widespread concern about the use of ancient, and often fragile, tracks by motorbikes, quad bikes and 4x4s. In particular, views were sought on the existing principle that permits use by modern motor vehicles on the basis that the routes were once used by horse-drawn carriages. The Government published its response to the consultation, alongside the results of a Defra research report on the use of byways open to all traffic by motor vehicles. Over 14,000 responses were received to the consultation. The full response, *The Government's framework for action*, and the Defra research report are published online at www.defra.gov.uk/ wildlife-countryside/cl/mpv/index.htm.

17 DISABILITY DISCRIMINATION BILL

The Disability Discrimination Bill was introduced into the House of Lords on 25 November 2004. The Bill will make major changes to the existing law, affecting employers, landlords and managers of rented premises, passenger rail operators, larger private clubs, general qualifications bodies, publishers of advertisements, as well as giving public authorities a duty to promote equality of opportunity for disabled people when exercising their functions.

In particular, landlords or managers of rented premises will come under a duty to take reasonable steps to provide auxiliary aids or services to enable a disabled person to occupy the rented premises, or to modify any practices or policies which make it unreasonably difficult for a disabled person to occupy the rented premises. This does not, however, extend to being required to remove or alter any physical features.

There are changes to the definition of disability. A mental illness will no longer have to be a 'clinically well recognised' one to qualify, and people with cancer, HIV or MS will be deemed to be 'disabled', even before the onset of symptoms affecting normal day-to-day activities.

18 REAL ESTATE INVESTMENT TRUSTS

In his pre-Budget report on 2 December 2004, the Chancellor ruled out legislating for the establishment of Real Estate Investment Trusts ('REITS') prior to 2006 at the earliest.

In March 2003, the Chancellor expressed his intention to 'explore with the industry evidence for the effectiveness of further measures to improve the efficiency and flexibility of commercial real estate'. This led to the Government launching a consultation on the proposed introduction of a new form of property investment fund, equivalent to REITS, which are common to many economies around the world – most notably the U.S.A., Australia, Japan and France. The consultation document was issued in response to concerns that the tax system was contributing to distortions in the market for property investment, resulting in poor liquidity, barriers to entering the market and higher debt financing levels.

If established, REITS would be expected to be exempt from capital gains tax and tax on property rental income. In return, the funds would to required to distribute most of their profits in the form of dividends. Any property company wanting to convert to a REIT would be likely to have to pay tax on inherent gains, referred to as a 'conversion charge'.

The Government had expressed the hope that the introduction of REITS would lead to a more efficient and flexible property market in the UK, accessible by the private sector and fair to all taxpayers, while at the same time not reducing the overall tax revenue from the property investment markets. The broad objective would be to create a new property investment vehicle that offers after-tax returns more closely aligned to those achieved from holding property directly. The consultation document outlined a variety of possible features and choices on which responses were sought by mid-July 2004. The Government received around 250 responses.

The pre-Budget report issued by the Treasury contains only two paragraphs on REITS, and this may reflect a downgrading of the Government's priorities in this area. The report states that the Government is continuing to explore whether the introduction of REITS would meet its objectives; that it continues to believe that tax reform in this area has the potential to improve the efficiency of the property market, and that it will report back with a discussion paper by Budget 2005 for further dialogue with industry representatives.

19   *PRE-BUDGET STATEMENT: PROPERTY TAX*

The pre-Budget report on 2 December 2004 contained a number of property tax items:

a) The option to tax

To coincide with the pre-Budget Report, the Government launched a consultation on the circumstances in which an owner of property who has 'opted to tax' may subsequently choose to revoke that option.

Revocation would result in exempt supplies then being made. This is of particular significance to landlords who let their properties to tenants carrying an exempt or partially exempt businesses (such as banks and other financial institutions) for whom VAT is wholly or partially irrecoverable. A landlord who is entitled to revoke could agree to do so for an uplift in rents if this would be advantageous to his tenant. As against this the landlord must weigh the effect on irrecoverable VAT.

Legislation currently allows an election to be revoked, where 20 years or more have passed since the election took effect, and Customs' consent to the revocation is obtained.

The option to tax was first introduced with effect from August 1989. Revocations will therefore become possible as from August 2009. The consultation is intended to help the Government decide in what circumstances they will allow a property owner to revoke an election or, indeed, whether the right to revoke should be withdrawn.

New legislation might include:

- provision for the right to revoke to be available automatically if certain conditions are fulfilled;

- early revocation (in other words, before the 20-year time limit) in certain circumstances;

- conditions to the right to revoke. In this respect, not all tenants will benefit if a landlord can simply revoke his option and then raise rents to compensate for his loss of input tax recovery; and

- anti-avoidance provisions.

Further details and information can be found at www.hmce.gov.uk.

b) Business Property Renovation Allowance

Subject to State Aid approval by the European Commission, as well as a consultation period up to 1 March 2005, the Government proposes to introduce the Business Property Renovation Allowance scheme ('BPRA'). Under this scheme the renovation or conversion of a business property, situated in a designated disadvantaged area and vacant for the past 12 months, will qualify for 100% capital allowances for the capital costs of that renovation or conversion.

This is a measure to foster regeneration in specified disadvantaged areas of the UK, by encouraging enterprise and economic activity in those areas.

It is proposed that BPRA can be claimed by a person with a legal interest in a *qualifying building* and who incurs *qualifying expenditure* in order to create *qualifying business premises*. These are explained as follows:

Qualifying expenditure – BPRA will be available for a period of five years only. To qualify, expenditure must be incurred in this period. In addition, expenditure on the following will not qualify:

i)   the acquisition of land or rights over land;

ii) building extensions;

iii) development of adjoining land; and

iv) the provision of plant and machinery (unless it becomes a fixture).

Qualifying building – this refers to a building which is situated in one of the designated disadvantaged areas and which:

i)   has been unused for a year or longer;

ii) was last used for a business purpose; and

iii) is the whole building (special rules apply for parts of buildings).

The designated disadvantaged areas are the same areas as those designated for the purposes of Stamp Duty Land Tax.

Qualifying business premises – the end result of the expenditure must be that a building is brought back into productive use or, if the premises has been renovated for leasing, the premises must be suitable, ready and held out for letting for business purposes.

There are two forms of allowances available, initial allowances and writing-down allowances:

Initial allowances – A person qualifying for BPRA can claim a 100% up-front tax relief for the capital costs of the renovation or conversion, which can be set off against the taxable profits of that person in the tax year in which the expenditure was incurred. A person does not have to claim the entire 100% relief. A partial claim may be preferable where that person has insufficient profits against which to set the relief.

Writing-down allowances – If a person does not claim the entire initial allowance, in subsequent years a claim for further writing-down allowances can be made at the rate of 25% of the balance of the unrelieved expenditure, provided that that person retains the relevant interest in the premises and they continue to constitute qualifying business premises.

As with capital allowances in general, allowances are the subject of claw back in certain circumstances, essentially if within seven years of the renovation the person sells the relevant interest, grants a long lease, or demolishes the qualifying building.

c) Chargeable gains

As a result of legislation introduced by the Finance Act 2003, which partially disapplied the market value rule in the context of certain options, it became possible to transfer investment property at an undervalue in circumstances where the gain (or loss) was calculated by reference to the actual consideration paid. This allowed inherent gains to be 'exported' or transferred to a tax favoured entity, therefore avoiding tax.

The Chancellor has announced that changes will be introduced to counter such schemes. The new rules will apply in relation to options exercised on or after 2 December 2004.

d) Corporation tax reform

The Government has proposed the creation of a new 'operating business' source of income that will bring together trading and letting income, together with miscellaneous income, under one single charge to tax. Currently, the schedular system requires companies to pigeonhole profits and losses into separate categories; losses from one activity cannot always be offset against profits from another.

If the proposal is implemented then there will be one set of operating loss rules, allowing a loss to be offset against:

i) other profits (including capital gains) in the accounting period in which the loss arises;

ii) the total profits for the previous 12 months;

iii) the total profits of other members of the company's group in the same period; or

iv) future profits of the operating business.

The Government has warned that anti-avoidance provisions will be introduced to prevent companies abusing the new regime. Changes may also be made to the availability of pre-commencement losses, but these will only apply to such losses arising after the introduction of the reforms; losses which have already arisen will continue to be treated under the existing rules.

The Government is also considering amendments to the capital allowances legislation. It has rejected the proposal that capital allowances be abolished with the tax treatment of capital expenditure instead following accounting practice. Nor will relief be made available in 2005 for abortive capital transaction costs, although the Government is considering possible means of achieving this.

It is also proposed that capital allowances which have previously been available to landlords under certain leases (referred to in the draft legislation as 'long funding leases') will now be available to the tenant only, with the result that leasing transactions will be less commercially attractive in future. The change will apply equally to fixtures.

Further details and information can be found at www.inlandrevenue.gov.uk.

20   HOME INFORMATION PACKS

Under the Housing Act 2004, from 2007 homeowners or their selling agents will be required to have a home information pack when marketing homes for sale, and to make a copy of the pack available to prospective buyers on request. The Act will also require estate agents, who are marketing homes for sale, to belong to an approved redress scheme. Legislation to introduce the home information pack was first introduced in the Homes Bill on 12 December 2000. That Bill was unable to complete its passage before Parliament was dissolved for the 2001 General Election. Legislation was reintroduced as part of the Housing Bill, which became an Act on 18 November 2004.

The home information pack is likely to include the following documents, most of which are currently provided later in the sale:

● Terms of sale.

● Evidence of title.

- Replies to standard preliminary enquiries made on behalf of buyers.

- Copies of any planning, listed building and building regulations consents and approvals.

- For new properties, copies of warranties and guarantees.

- Any guarantees for work carried out on the property.

- Replies to local searches.

- A home condition report based on a professional survey of the property, including an energy efficiency assessment.

Also, for leasehold properties:

- A copy of the lease.

- Most recent service charge accounts and receipts.

- Building insurance policy details and payment receipts.

- Regulations made by the landlord or management company.

- Memorandum and articles of the landlord or management company.

The Government anticipates making regulations regarding the contents of the home information pack, any exceptions to the duty to provide a pack and for the home condition report in Summer 2005. In Autumn 2005, the certification scheme for home inspectors should be approved in readiness to issue licenses early in 2006. In Summer 2006 there will be a national voluntary 'dry run' of the home information pack leading in, early 2007, to the introduction of the home information pack. From 2007, estate agents and others marketing homes for sale will be required to have a home information pack and to provide copies to potential buyers on request.

Failure to provide a home information pack will not be a criminal offence. The enforcement regime will be based on civil sanctions, and will give local weights and measures authorities primary responsibility for enforcing the home information pack obligations. Trading Standards Officers would be given discretion to determine appropriate action in each case – whether to provide information and assistance, issue a warning or a civil fixed penalty notice. The penalty would be set at a rate determined by the Secretary of State (initially envisaged to be around £200). Trading Standards Officers would also be able to notify the Office of Fair Trading of any breach by persons acting as an estate agent, which could also trigger action by the OFT under Estate Agents Act 1979. Trading Standards Officers would also have a duty to notify any breach where a fixed penalty notice had been issued. The Government is consulting The Law Society about ways of applying equivalent enforcement arrangements to conveyancers marketing properties for sale. In addition, a person who breached the home information pack obligations would be liable to be sued by prospective buyers for recovery of the costs of obtaining documents which should have been provided in the pack.

To help ensure a smooth and successful implementation of the statutory home information pack scheme, the intention is to facilitate a 'dry run' of the scheme on a voluntary basis in England and Wales from July 2006. The aim of the 'dry run' is to provide the industry and the public with the opportunity to experience and operate the full statutory home information packs scheme in advance of its introduction throughout England and Wales on a mandatory basis. It is envisaged that the 'dry run' will provide an opportunity for the industry to operate the full home information pack scheme ahead of statutory introduction, prepare the home buying and selling public for the new system, and allow Government and industry to identify and address any outstanding problems.

Part E

REFERENCE SECTION

1.1 **Dilapidations: The Modern Law and Practice**
Author: Nicholas Dowding and Kirk Reynolds
Publisher: Sweet & Maxwell

1.2 **Garner's Local Land Charges, 13th Edition**
Author: Jan E Boothroyd
Publisher: Shaw & Sons

1.3 **Service Charges and Management**
Author: Philip Rainey, Paul Staddon and Lisa A Sinclair
Publisher: Sweet & Maxwell

1.4 **Boundaries and Easements: 1st Supplement**
Author: Colin Sara
Publisher: Sweet & Maxwell

1.5 **Plural Ownership**
Author: Roger J Smith
Publisher: Oxford University Press

1.6 **Business Tenancies: A Practical Guide to the Changes to the Landlord and Tenant Act 1954 Pt II**
Author: Jacqui Joyce
Publisher: Legalease

1.7 **Butterworth's Business Landlord and Tenant Handbook**
Author: Paul Matthews and Katie Bradford
Publisher: Butterworths Law

1.8 **Planning and Compulsory Purchase Act 2004**
Author: Stephen Tromans, Martin Edwards, Richard Harwood and Justine Thornton
Publisher: Law Society Publications

1.9 Tolley's Property Taxes
Author: Robert W Maas
Publisher: Tolley Publishing

1.10 Land Law
Author: Margaret Wilkie, Peter Luxton and Rosalind Malcolm
Publisher: Oxford University Press

1.11 Landlord and Tenant
Author: Mark Pawlowski and James Brown
Publisher: Oxford University Press

1.12 Gadsden on Commons and Greens
Author: Edward Cousins and Nicholas Le Poidevin
Publisher: Sweet & Maxwell

1.13 Guide to the National Conveyancing Protocol: TransAction 2004
Publisher: Law Society Publications

1.14 Renewal of Business Tenancies: 1st Supplement
Author: Kirk Reynolds and Wayne Clark
Publisher: Sweet & Maxwell

1.15 Preston and Newsom: Restrictive Covenants Affecting Freehold Land
Author: G Newsom
Publisher: Sweet & Maxwell

1.16 Flat Owner's Guide
Author: Paul Walentowicz
Publisher: Shelter

1.17 Land: The Law of Real Property
Author: Cedric D Bell
Publisher: Old Bailey Press

1.18 Property Law and Practice
Author: P Butt
Publisher: College of Law

1.19 Elements of Land Law
Author: Kevin J Gray and Susan Francis Gray
Publisher: Butterworths Law

1.20 Conveyancer's Money Laundering Compliance Guide
Author: Robert David Montague and Christine Montague
Publisher: The Legal Workshop Ltd

1.21 Anstey's Boundary Disputes
Author: David Powell
Publisher: RICS

1.22 Conveyancing Handbook
Author: Frances Silverman
Publisher: Law Society Publications

1.23 Blackstone's Statutes on Property Law
Author: Meryl Thomas
Publisher: Oxford University Press

1.24 Conveyancing Law
Author: Andrew Walker
Publisher: Old Bailey Press

1.25 IHT and Private Property
Author: Emma Chamberlain
Publisher: Butterworths Law

1.26 Galbraith's Building and Land Management Law
Author: Anne Galbraith *et al*
Publisher: Butterworth-Heinemann

1.27 Sweet & Maxwell's Property Law Statutes
Author: Nigel P Gravells
Publisher: Sweet & Maxwell

1.28 Making Sense of Land Law
Author: April Stroud
Publisher: Butterworths Law

1.29 Tolley's Trust and Estate Practitioner Checklists
Author: John Thurston
Publisher: Tolley Publishing

1.30 Practical Approach to Landlord and Tenant
Author: Simon Garner and Alexandra Frith
Publisher: Oxford University Press

1.31 Practical Approach to Conveyancing
Author: Robert M Abbey and Mark B Richards
Publisher: Oxford University Press

1.32 Property Law & Practice
Author: Russell Hewitson and Phillip H Kenny
Publisher: Northumbria Law Press

1.33 Land Law: Text and Materials
Author: Nigel P Gravells
Publisher: Sweet & Maxwell

1.34 Hedge Height and Light Loss
Publisher: Office of the Deputy Prime Minister

1.35 Letting Business Premises
Author: Trevor M Aldridge
Publisher: Sweet & Maxwell

1.36 Business Tenancies: A Guide to the New Law
Author: Jason Hunter
Publisher: Law Society Publications

1.37 Dixon on Land Law
Author: Martin Dixon
Publisher: Cavendish Publishing Ltd

1.38 Land Law
Author: Michael Haley
Publisher: Sweet & Maxwell

1.39 Textbook on Land Law
Author: Judith-Anne MacKenzie and Mary Phillips
Publisher: Oxford University Press

2 ARTICLES

2.1 A Bow Without a String?
Author: Dean Underwood
Topic: Demotion orders
148 SJ 771

2.2 **A Bridge Over Troubled Waters**
Author: Simon Catterrall
Topic: *Waters v Welsh Development Agency* [2004] UKHL 19;
[2004] 2 All ER 915
Estates Gazette, 3 July 2004, p 120

2.3 **A Healthier Alternative**
Authors: Catriona Smith and Peter Reekie
Topic: Proposals to amend the Landlord and Tenant Act 1954
Estates Gazette, 28 February 2004, p 136

2.4 **A Meaningful Glance at Fixtures and Fittings**
Author: Hazel Williamson
Estates Gazette, 10 January 2004, p 87

2.5 **A Procedure Guaranteed to Confuse**
Authors: Katharine Fenn, Allyson Colby and Sue Highmore
Topic: Contracting out of the security of tenure rules by guarantors
Estates Gazette, 19 June 2004, p 166

2.6 **A Recipe for Disaster**
Author: Katharine Fenn
Topic: Proposals to introduce prescribed information in registrable leases
Estates Gazette, 20 November 2004, p 159

2.7 **A Valid Application**
Author: Sandi Murdoch
Topic: *Norwich Union Linked Life Assurance Ltd v Mercantile Credit Co Ltd* [2003] All ER (D) 376 (Dec)
Estates Gazette, 21 August 2004, p 133

2.8 **Accommodating Families With Children – The Final Chapter**
Author: Sonia Rai
[2004] JHL 21

2.9 **Adapting to Change**
Author: Clara Wright
Topic: E-conveyancing
148 SJ 249

2.10 Adequate Reasons
Author: Stephen Cattle
Topic: *South Buckinghamshire DC v Porter (No 2)* [2004] UKHL 33;
[2004] 1 WLR 1953
148 SJ 989

2.11 Agriculture Farm Tenancy Schemes – Transactions at Undervalue
Author: Adam Ibrahim and Sean Barton
(2004) 8 L & T Rev 77

2.12 An End of the Affair – Social Housing, Relationship Breakdown, and the Human Rights Act 1998
Authors: Martin Davis and David Hughes
[2004] Conv 19

2.13 Anti-avoidance and Land
Authors: B Kundu and G Beaumont
Tax Journal, Issue 747, p 11

2.14 Anti-social Behaviour Act 2003 and Gypsies, Travellers and Public Gatherings
Author: Timothy Baldwin
LA, August 2004, p 19

2.15 Anti-social Behaviour: More Ammunition for Landlords
Authors: S Beecham and A Rowley
Topic: The Anti-social Behaviour Act 2003 Pt II (ss 12-17)
154 NLJ 422

2.16 Avoiding the Elephant Traps
Author: Stephen Tromans
Topic: Environmental impact assessments
154 NLJ 60

2.17 Bankruptcy and Conveyancing
Author: Martin Tomsett
Topic: Buying property from a trustee in bankruptcy
148 SJ 286

2.18 Behind the Service Line
Authors: Ted Mercer and Christopher Bell
Topic: Leases which restrict choice of telecommunications operator
Estates Gazette, 11 December 2004, p 77

2.19 Beneficial Joint Tenants and the Protection of Purchasers: An Unsolved Problem
Author: E J Cooke
[2004] Conv 41

2.20 Building a Case for a Single Notice
Author: Douglas Readings
Topic: *Long Acre Securities Ltd v Karet* [2004] EWHC 442 (Ch); [2004] 11 EG 138 (CS)
154 NLJ 622

2.21 Business Lease Renewals and the Courts
Author: Debra Mo
154 NLJ 1620

2.22 Business Tenancies Reforms – Should We Have Expected More?
Author: John Martin
(2004) 8 L & T Rev 52

2.23 Causing a Nuisance
Author: Justin Valentine
Topic: Disability discrimination and possession proceedings by social landlords against mentally ill tenants on the ground of causing a nuisance
148 SJ 372

2.24 Challenging Negative Determinations under Section 55 of the Nationality, Immigration and Asylum Act 2002
Author: Sally Blackmore
[2004] JHL 60

2.25 Charities
Author: Reg Nock
Topic: Charities and Stamp Duty Land Tax
Tax Journal, Issue 759, p 11

2.26 Clamping Down on Avoidance
Author: Simon Swann
Topic: Avoidance of Stamp Duty Land Tax
Tax Journal, Issue 759, p 8

2.27 Commercial Lease Shake-up
Author: L Raymond and A Boulton
154 NLJ 1386

2.28 Common Ground
Author: Stephen Murch
Topic: The components of commonhold
154 NLJ 1246, 1327

2.29 Commonhold
Author: James Driscoll
148 SJ 1046, 1082, 1112, 1146

2.30 Commonhold – Not So Much flawed, But Different
Author: Richard Frost
154 NLJ 330

2.31 Consultation Requirements – The New Regime
Author: Natalie Hourihan
Topic: The Service Charges (Consultation Requirements) (England)
Regulations 2003, SI 2003/1987
(2004) 8 L & T Rev 23, 49

2.32 Controlling Asbestos in the Workplace and Beyond
Author: Andrew Morgan
Topic: The Control of Asbestos at Work Regulations 2002, SI 2002/2675
(2004) 8 L & T Rev 55

2.33 County Court Powers in Housing Appeals
Author: Tony Harrop-Griffiths
Topic: *O'Connor v Kensington & Chelsea LBC* [2004] EWCA Civ 394;
[2004] All ER (D) 552 (Mar)
154 NLJ 860

2.34 County Court Powers in Housing Appeals
Author: Robin Levett
154 NLJ 916

2.35 Crying Out for Reform
Author: Martin Edwards
Topic: *Waters v Welsh Development Agency* [2004] UKHL 19;
[2004] 1 WLR 1304
148 SJ 613

2.36 Deciding Factor
Author: Jon Holbrook
Topic: The appeal notice in homelessness cases
148 SJ 864

2.37 Decline of the Adverse Possessors
Author: Paul Letman
154 NLJ 740

2.38 Defining Partnership Transactions?
Author: Sharron Carle
Topic: Stamp Duty Land Tax and partnership transactions
Tax Journal, Issue 759, p 14

2.39 Develop a Good Sense of Right and Wrong
Author: Monica Dawson
Topic: Misrepresentation by planning developers
Estates Gazette, 30 October 2004, p 148

**2.40 Developments that Cause a Nuisance: the Legal
Significance of the Grant of Planning Permission**
Author: Alec Samuels
[2004] JPL 394

2.41 Dilapidations – A Further Look at the Protocol
Author: J Joyce and K Conway
Topic: The Dilapidations Protocol
154 NLJ 1805

2.42 Discrimination, Rented Housing and the Law
Author: Helen Carr
154 NLJ 454

2.43 Dispose of with Care
Author: Stephen O'Brien

Topic: Disposals of incomplete developments
Estates Gazette, 27 November 2004, p 128

2.44 Disrepair Disputes
Author: Debra Mo
Topic: The Pre-Action Protocol for Housing Disrepair Cases
148 SJ 739

2.45 Disrepair or Damp?
Author: Debra Mo
148 SJ 458

2.46 Dust-Buster
Author: Neil Toner
Topic: The Control of Asbestos at Work Regulations 2002, SI 2002/2675
The Lawyer, 16 February 2004, p RE3

2.47 Environmental Impact Assessment: What's Next?
Author: Richard Harwood
[2004] JPL 1161

2.48 Extra Vehicular Activity
Author: Chiara Drukarz Kantor
Topic: Vehicle access
LS Gaz, 24 June 2004, p 30

2.49 Fence Over the River Kwai – A Comparative View of Noticing under the Electronic Communications Code Considered against Planning Noticing under the Permitted Development Orders through a Review of a Recent Case
Author: Joanna Tansley
Topic: *Lloyd Jones v T Mobile (UK) Ltd* [2003] EWCA Civ 1162; [2003] All ER (D) 561 (Jul)
[2004] JPL 273

2.50 Follow the Letter of the Law
Author: Allyson Colby, Andrew Wallis and Katharine Fenn
Topic: Contracting business leases out of the Landlord and Tenant Act 1954
Estates Gazette, 29 May 2004, p 132

2.51 **For Crown and Country**
Author: Gill Castorina
Topic: The extent to which the Planning and Compulsory Purchase Bill is binding on the Crown
Estates Gazette, 31 January 2004, p 141

2.52 **Getting Demotion Right**
Author: D Underwood and J Holbrook
Topic: Demotion orders under the Anti-social Behaviour Act 2003
154 NLJ 1080, 1224

2.53 **Grand Designs**
Author: Mark Smulian
Topic: Planning law reform
LS Gaz, 12 February 2004, p 24

2.54 **Green and Pleasant**
Author: David Danskin
Topic: *R (on the application of Beresford) v Sunderland CC* [2003] UKHL 60; [2004] 1 All ER 160
147 SJ 162

2.55 **Growing Pains**
Author: Peter Williams
Topic: The Land Registration Act 2002
Estates Gazette, 16 October 2004, p 152

2.56 **Home Truths**
Author: Alastair Redpath-Stevens
Topic: *Osmani v Harrow LBC* [2004] UKHL 4; [2004] All ER (D) 64 (Feb)
148 SJ 246

2.57 **Horror Homes**
Author: Mark Pawlowski
Topic: *Sykes v Taylor-Rose* [2004] EWCA Civ 299; [2004] All ER (D) 468 (Feb)
148 SJ 497

2.58 **Housing Act 2004**
Author: Christopher Baker
148 SJ 1384, 1454

2.59 **Illegality and Prescription**
Author: David Fox
[2004] Conv 173

2.60 **Illuminating Ruminations on a Disappearing Issue**
Author: Hazel Williamson
Topic: Rights of light
Estates Gazette, 6 November 2004, p 119

2.61 **Immovable Property – Immovable VAT Rules**
Author: Martin Scammell
Topic: EU accession, real property and VAT
Tax Journal, Issue 738, p 11

2.62 **In With the New, Out With the Old**
Author: Jonathan Cantor
Topic: The termination and renewal of leases of business premises
LS Gaz, 24 June 2004, p 29

2.63 **Into the Sidings?**
Author: Martin Edwards
Topic: *R (on the application of Wells) v Secretary of State for Transport, Local Government and the Regions* (Case C-201/02) [2004] All ER (D) 04 (Jan), ECJ
148 SJ 200

2.64 **Is Stamp Taxes Planning Dead?**
Author: Steven McGrady
Tax Journal, Issue 759, p 17

2.65 **Is this an Excess of Access?**
Author: Peter Hemens
Topic: The requirement to make buildings accessible for disabled persons
Estates Gazette, 17 January 2004, p 98

2.66 **It's Fair Play for Property Consumers**
Author: David Lowe and Verity Chase
Topic: The application of the unfair contract terms legislation to property transactions
Estates Gazette, 11 December 2004, p 74

2.67 **Land Registration for Litigators**
Author: Linda Chamberlain
Topic: The Land Registration Rules 2003, SI 2003/1417
148 SJ 283

2.68 **Lessee-Owned Blocks: Moving Towards Commonhold**
Author: James Brenan
(2004) 8 L & T Rev 2

2.69 **Long and Short of It**
Author: Emma Slessenger
Topic: Underleases for the whole term
Estates Gazette, 27 November 2004, p 127

2.70 **Major Housing Developments: Density and Design in
Appeal Decisions 2000-03**
Author: Angela Hull
[2004] JPL 379

2.71 **Making Plans**
Author: Robert McCracken and Gregory Jones
Topic: The Planning and Compulsory Purchase Act 2004
148 SJ 1296, 1337, 1395

2.72 **New Act Blossoms Forth**
Author: Martin Edwards and John Martin
Topic: The Planning and Compulsory Purchase Act 2004
Estates Gazette, 16 October 2004, p 158

2.73 **New Consultation on Termination of Tenancies for Tenant
Default**
Author: Mark Pawlowski
(2004) 8 L & T Rev 32

2.74 **No Room for Confusion**
Author: Gill Castorina
Topic: Drafting planning permission conditions
Estates Gazette, 4 September 2004, p 120

2.75 **Non-Resident Landlords Scheme**
Author: James Paterson
Tax Journal, Issue 726, p 9

2.76   **Off the Register**
Author: Alan Riley
Topic: Whether landlords are required to register lease variations
148 SJ 340

2.77   **Overstepping the Mark**
Author: Alan Harrison
Topic: Councillors making prejudicial planning decisions
148 SJ 1054

2.78   **Planning for the 21st Century**
Author: Gary Sector
154 NLJ 1578, 1697

2.79   **Planning on Change**
Author: Robert McCracken
Topic: The Planning and Compulsory Purchase Bill
148 SJ 226

2.80   **Poor Law and Poor Houses**
Author: John Spencer
168 JP Jo 420

2.81   **Possession Claims**
Author: John Platt
Topic: *Day v Coltrane* [2003] EWCA Civ 342; [2003] 1 WLR 1379
154 NLJ 1470

2.82   **Preliminary Points Often in Arbitration**
Author: Michele Freyne
Topic: *Beegas Nominees Ltd v Decco Ltd* [2003] EWHC 1891 (Ch);
[2003] 43 EG 138
[2004] 8 L &T Rev 5

2.83   **Prescription – What is it For?**
Author: Colin Sara
[2004] Conv 13

2.84   **Prescriptive Framework**
Author: Julie Jenkins
Topic: Proposals to introduce prescribed information in registrable leases
Estates Gazette, 20 November 2004, p 156

2.85 Property and the Budget
Author: Charles Beer
Tax Journal, Issue 734, p 11

2.86 Property Disposals and Valuations on Tax Returns
Author: Tim Lyford
Tax Journal, Issue 742, p 9

2.87 Property Investment Funds
Author: Helen Demuth
Tax Journal, Issue 742, p 7

2.88 Real Estate as Security Following the Land Registration Act 2002
Author: Trevor Moore
(2004) 2 JIBFL 56

2.89 Relieve Landlords of an Unnecessary Burden
Author: Emma Humphreys
Topic: The rules relating to the redevelopment of premises
Estates Gazette, 29 May 2004, p 135

2.90 Renting Homes
Author: Martin Partington
[2004] JHL 9

2.91 Renting Homes – New Opportunities: A Personal View
Author: Martin Partington
(2004) 8 L & T Rev 26

2.92 Residential Conveyancing: A Special Case
Author: Michael Garson
154 NLJ 102

2.93 Restricted Range of Protection
Author: Philip Roberts
Topic: The protection of third-party rights in registered titles
Estates Gazette, 16 October 2004, p 154

2.94 Restricting the Underlease Terms
Author: John West
Topic: Restrictions on subletting
(2004) 8 L & T Rev 8

2.95 Rewriting the Form Book on Leases
Author: Julie Jenkins
Topic: The way details are presented in lease applications
LS Gaz, 25 November 2004, p 34

2.96 Rules of Engagement
Author: Grania Langdon-Down
Topic: The relationship between solicitors and mortgage lenders
LS Gaz, 16 September 2004, p 20

2.97 Squatters' Rights
Author: William Hanbury
Topic: Adverse possession claims during the transition from the Limitation Act 1980 to the Land Registration Act 2002
148 SJ 141

2.98 Stamp Duty Land Tax and Fraud
Author: Patrick Cannon
Tax Journal, Issue 730, p 11

2.99 Stamp Duty Land Tax
Author: Mike Boutell
Topic: Implementation of Stamp Duty Land Tax
Tax Journal, Issue 742, p 13

2.100 Stamp Duty Land Tax – A Guide for Charities
Author: Carolyn Owen
New Law Journal Charities Appeals Supplement, 2004, p 22

2.101 Stamping Out Partnerships
Author: K Griffin and G West
Topic: Partnerships' liability to Stamp Duty Land Tax
Tax Journal, Issue 754, p 9

2.102 Strange Goings-On
Author: Hazel Williamson
Topic: Enfranchisement
Estates Gazette, 13 November 2004, p 142

2.103 Succession of Tenancies for Same-sex Couples: More Confusion Ahead?
Author: Sarah Blandy
[2004] JHL 51

2.104 Tenant-Friendly
Author: Jeremy Hudson
Topic: *Howard de Walden Estates Ltd v Malekshad* [2003] EWHC 3106 (Ch); [2003] All ER (D) 413 (Dec)
148 SJ 220

2.105 Thanks for the Clarifications
Author: Gordon Keenay
Topic: Stamp Duty Land Tax and charging provisions
Tax Journal, Issue 759, p 5

2.106 That Will Do Nicely
Author: John Hayward
Topic: Ending the impact of Stamp Duty Land Tax on pension schemes
Tax Journal, Issue 727, p 17

2.107 The Brave New World of Planning
Author: Michael Gallimore
Topic: The Planning and Compulsory Purchase Act 2004
Estates Gazette, 17 July 2004, p 108

2.108 The Bricks and Mortar of Reform
Author: Stephen Murch
Topic: Business tenancy reforms
154 NLJ 170

2.109 The End of the Line Forfeiture
Author: Jacqui Joyce
Topic: Proposals to reform the law of repossession
Estates Gazette, 14 February 2004, p 122

2.110 The Importance of Alternative Proposals in Development Control
Author: Stephen Whale
[2004] JPL 887

2.111 The Murky Ground of Village Greens
Author: Julia Berry and Emma Cawley
Estates Gazette, 10 January 2004, p 84

2.112 The New Electronic Age
Author: Allyson Colby
Topic: E-conveyancing
Estates Gazette, 16 October 2004, p 155

2.113 The New Regime of Business Tenancy Renewal
Author: John Furber
154 NLJ 796

2.114 The Planning and Compulsory Purchase Act 2004
Author: David Elvin
[2004] JPL 1339

2.115 The Planning and Compulsory Purchase Act 2004: The Final Cut
Author: Pat Thomas
[2004] JPL 1348

2.116 The Purity of Commonholds
Author: P F Smith
Topic: The relationship between the leasehold and commonhold systems
[2004] Conv 194

2.117 The Return of an Older Era
Author: Michael Metliss and Charlotte Bijlani
Topic: Lease renewal
Estates Gazette, 13 November 2004, p 145

2.118 Time to Clean Up Your Act
Author: Michael Gallimore
Topic: Strategic environmental assessments
Estates Gazette, 18 September 2004, p 159

2.119 Toleration or Licence – When is Land Used 'As of Right'
Author: S Warfield and J Holroyd
154 NLJ 122

2.120 Twists and Terms
Author: Edward Bannister
Topic: The interpretation of ambiguous rent review clauses
Estates Gazette, 12 June 2004, p 140

2.121 U-Turn on Rights of Way
Author: Stephen Bickford-Smith and Camilla Lamont
Topic: *Bakewell Management Ltd v Brandwood* [2004] UKHL 14;
[2004] 2 All ER 305
148 SJ 455

2.122 Using the Disrepair Protocol
Author: W Backhouse and D Forbes
Topic: The housing disrepair pre-action protocol
[2004] JHL 25

2.123 Valuation for Diminution in the Landlord's Reversion
Author: Peter Beckett
(2004) 8 L &T Rev 73

2.124 VAT and the Property Cycle
Author: John Voyez
Tax Journal, Issue 742, p 19

2.125 What are the Options?
Author: Peter Williams
Topic: Upwards-only rent reviews
Estates Gazette, 19 June 2004, p 162

2.126 Why Landlords must Proceed with Care
Author: Jason Hunter
Topic: Tenancies excluded from the Landlord and Tenant Act 1954
LS Gaz, 4 June 2004, p 35

3	WEB SITES

3.1 PARLIAMENT

3.1.1 www.parliament.uk
UK Parliamentary site

3.1.2 www.parliament.uk/about_commons/about_commons.cfm
House of Commons

3.1.3 www.parliament.uk/about_lords/about_lords.cfm
House of Lords

3.2　LEGISLATION

3.2.1　www.hmso.gov.uk/acts.htm
UK Acts of Parliament

3.2.2　www.hmso.gov.uk/stat.htm
UK Statutory Instruments

3.2.3　www.hmso.gov.uk
HM Stationery Office

3.3　GOVERNMENT DEPARTMENTS

3.3.1　www.ukonline.gov.uk
The entry site for all government websites

3.3.2　www.homeoffice.gov.uk
Home Office

3.3.3　www.hmce.gov.uk
HM Customs & Excise

3.3.4　www.inlandrevenue.gov.uk/home.htm
HM Inland Revenue

3.3.5　www.dca.gov.uk
Department for Constitutional Affairs

3.3.6　www.insolvency.gov.uk
The Insolvency Service

3.3.7　www.treasury.gov.uk
HM Treasury

3.3.8　www.odpm.gov.uk
Office of the Deputy Prime Minister

3.3.9　www.defra.gov.uk
Department for Environment, Food and Rural Affairs

3.3.10　www.charity-commission.gov.uk
The Charity Commission

3.3.11　www.lawcom.gov.uk
The Law Commission

3.3.12 www.courtservice.gov.uk
The Court Service

3.3.13 www.courtservice.gov.uk/tribunals/lands_frm.htm
Lands Tribunal decisions

3.3.14 www.offsol.demon.co.uk
Official Solicitor

3.4   LAND REGISTRATION

3.4.1 www.landreg.gov.uk
HM Land Registry

3.4.2 www.landreg.gov.uk/e-conveyancing
HM Land Registry's e-conveyancing website

3.4.3 www.landreg.gov.uk/legislation
HM Land Registry's Land Registration Act website

3.4.4 www.landregistrydirect.gov.uk
Land Registry Direct

3.4.5 www.landregisteronline.gov.uk
Online service aimed at the general public.

3.4.6 www.landregistry.gov.uk/strategy
HM Land Registry strategy

3.4.7 www.egi.co.uk/propert-e
E-conveyancing site developed by EGi and Wragge & Co

3.5   PUBLISHERS

3.5.1 www.oup.co.uk/law
Oxford University Press

3.5.2 www.cavendishpublishing.com
Cavendish Publishing

3.5.3 www.butterworths.com
Butterworths

3.5.4 www.smlawpub.co.uk
Sweet & Maxwell

3.5.5 www.shaws.co.uk
Shaw & Sons Ltd

3.5.6 **www.jordanpublishing.co.uk**
Jordan Publishing Ltd

3.6 **ONLINE LEGAL RESEARCH SERVICES**

3.6.1 **www.butterworths.com**
Butterworths LexisNexis Direct

3.6.2 **www.westlaw.co.uk**
Westlaw

3.6.3 **www.bailii.org**
British and Irish Legal Information Institute

3.6.4 **www.justis.com**
Justis

3.6.5 **www.lawtel.com**
Lawtel

3.6.6 **www.egi.co.uk**
Estates Gazette EGi

3.6.7 **www.egi.co.uk/practicepoints.asp**
Recent property law developments

3.6.8 **www.icclaw.com**
The International Centre for Commercial Law

3.6.9 **www.propertylawuk.net**
Property Law website

3.7 **PROFESSIONAL BODIES**

3.7.1 **www.lawsociety.org.uk**
The Law Society

3.7.2 **www.cml.org.uk**
Council of Mortgage Lenders

3.7.3 **www.rics.org.uk**
Royal Institution of Chartered Surveyors

3.7.4 **www.conveyancers.org.uk**
The Society of Licensed Conveyancers

3.7.5 **www.theclc.gov.uk**
The Council for Licensed Conveyancers

3.7.6   www.bpf.propertymall.com
British Property Federation

3.7.7   www.nhbc.co.uk
NHBC

3.7.8   www.sava.org.uk
Independent standard setting body for property practitioners

3.8   LEGAL PORTALS

3.8.1   www.venables.co.uk
Legal resources pages

3.8.2   www.infolaw.co.uk
UK legal gateway site

3.8.3   www.online-law.co.uk
Online law

3.8.4   www.lawontheweb.co.uk
Legal resources

3.9   CONVEYANCING SEARCHES AND ENQUIRIES

3.9.1   www.homecheck.co.uk
Free report service for buyers

3.9.2   www.nlis.org.uk
National Land Information Service

3.9.3   www.searchflow.co.uk; www.tmproperty.co.uk; www.transaction-online.co.uk
The three licence holders providing access to the NLIS hub

3.9.4   www.coal.gov.uk
Coal Authority

3.9.5   www.countrywidelegal.co.uk
Countrywide Legal Indemnities

3.9.6   www.home-envirosearch.com
Envirosearch

3.9.7   www.landmarkinfo.co.uk
Landmark Information Group

3.9.8   www.drainageandwater.co.uk
Drainage and water searches

3.9.9   property.practicallaw.com/0-103-2123
Commercial Property Standard Enquiries

3.10   MISCELLANEOUS

3.10.1   www.thetimes.co.uk
The Times

3.10.2   www.streetmap.co.uk
UK street maps

3.10.3   www.commercialleasecodeew.co.uk
Code of Practice for Commercial Leases

3.10.4   www.lurotbrand.co.uk/splinta/home.htm
SPLINTA (Sellers' Pack Law Is Not The Answer)

3.10.5   www.solicitors-online.com
Law Society's Directory

3.10.6   www.lawgazette.co.uk
Law Society's Gazette

3.10.7   webjcli.ncl.ac.uk
Web Journal of Current Legal Issues

3.10.8   www.lease-advice.org
The Leasehold Advisory Service

3.10.9   www.thelawyer.co.uk
The Lawyer

3.10.10   www.planningadvice.co.uk
Free planning law service

3.10.11   www.shelter.org.uk
Shelter

3.10.12   www.psa.co.uk/forum/index.asp
Legal property news and resources

3.10.13   www.landlordlaw.co.uk
Information and resources for landlords and tenants

3.10.14 www.lease-advice.org
The Leasehold Advisory Service

3.10.15 www.planningportal.gov.uk
The planning portal

3.10.16 www.copso.org.uk
The Council of Property Search Organisations

4	LAND REGISTRATION RULES 2003 – TABLE OF LAND REGISTRY FORMS

HM Land Registry Form Code	*Form*
ACD	Application for approval of a standard form of charge deed and allocation of official Land Registry reference
ADV1	Application for registration of a person in averse possession under Schedule 6 of the Land Registration Act 2002
ADV2	Application to be registered as a person to be notified of an application for adverse possession
AN1	Application to enter an agreed notice
AP1	Application to change the register
AS1	Assent of whole of registered title(s)
AS2	Assent of charge
AS3	Assent of part of registered title(s) by personal representative
CC	Entry of a note of consolidation of charges
CCD	Application to cancel a caution against dealings
CCT	Application to cancel a caution against first registration
CH1	Legal charge of a registered estate
CH2	Application to enter an obligation to make further advances
CH3	Application to note agreed maximum amount of security
CI	Certificate of inspection of title plan

CIT	Application in connection with court proceedings, insolvency and tax liability
CM1	Application to register a freehold estate in commonhold land
CM2	Application for the freehold estate to cease to be registered as a freehold estate in commonhold land during the transitional period
CM3	Application for the registration of an amended commonhold community statement and/or altered memorandum and articles of association
CM4	Application to add land to a commonhold registration
CM5	Application for the termination of a commonhold registration
CM6	Application for the registration of a successor commonhold association
CN1	Application to cancel a notice (other than a unilateral notice)
COE	Notification of change of extent of a commonhold unit over which there is a registered charge
CON1	Consent to the registration of land as commonhold land
CON2	Consent to an application for the freehold estate to cease to be registered as a freehold estate in commonhold land during the transitional period
COV	Application for registration with unit-holders
CS	Continuation sheet for use with application and disposal forms
CT1	Caution against first registration
DB	Application to determine the exact line of a boundary
DI	Disclosable overriding interests
DJP	Application to remove from the register the name of a deceased joint proprietor
DL	List of documents
DS1	Cancellation of entries relating to a charge
DS2	Application to cancel entries relating to a registered charge

DS3   Release of part of the land from a registered charge

EX1   Application for the registrar to designate a document as an exempt information document

EX1A   Reasons for exemption in support of an application to designate a document as an exempt information document

EX2   Application for official copy of an exempt information document

EX3   Application to remove the designation of a document as an exempt information document

FR1   First registration application

HC1   Application for copies of historical edition(s) of the register/title plan held in electronic form

ID1   Evidence of identity for a private individual

ID2   Evidence of identity for a corporate body

ID3   Evidence of identity for use with Forms RP2 or FR1 only

K001   Application for registration of a land charge

K002   Application for registration of a land charge of Class F

K003   Application for registration of a pending action

K004   Application for registration of a writ or order

K005   Application for registration of a deed of arrangement

K006   Application for registration of a priority notice

K007   Application for the renewal of a registration

K008   Application for the renewal of a registration of a land charge of Class F

K009   Application for the rectification of an entry in the register

K010   Continuation of an application

K011   Application to cancel an entry in the Land Charges Register (other than Class F)

K012   Application for cancellation of an entry in the register under special directions of The Registrar

K013   Application for cancellation of a land charge of Class F

K014   Declaration in support of an application for registration or rectification

K015	Application for an official search (not applicable to registered land)
K016	Application for an official search (bankruptcy only)
K019	Application for an office copy of an entry in the register
K020	Application for a certificate of the cancellation of an entry in the register
MH1	Application for registration of a notice of matrimonial rights
MH2	Application for renewal of registration in respect of matrimonial home rights
MH3	Application by mortgagee for official search in respect of matrimonial home rights
MH4	Cancellation of a Land Registry matrimonial home rights notice
NAP	Notice to the registrar in respect of an adverse possession application
OC1	Application for official copies of register/plan or certificate in Form CI
OC2	Application for official copies of documents only
OS1	Application by purchaser for official search without priority
OS2	Application by purchaser for official search without priority of part of land in a registered title or a pending first registration application
OS3	Application for official search without priority of the land in a registered title
PIC	Application for a personal inspection under s.66 of the Land Registration Act 2002
PN1	Application for a search in the index of proprietor's name
PRD1	Request for missing documents
PRD2	Notice to produce a document s.75 of the Land Registration Act 2002 and the Land Registration Rules 2003
RD1	Request for the return of original document(s)
RX1	Application to enter a restriction

RX2	Application for an order that a restriction be disapplied or modified
RX3	Application to cancel a restriction
RX4	Application to withdraw a restriction
SC	Application for noting the overriding priority of a statutory charge
SIF	Application for an official search of the index of relating franchises and manors
SIM	Application for an official search of the index map
SR1	Notice of surrender of development right(s)
TP1	Transfer of part of registered titles
TP2	Transfer of part of registered title(s) under power of sale
TP3	Transfer of portfolio of titles
TR1	Transfer of whole of registered title
TR2	Transfer of whole of registered title(s) under power of sale
TR3	Transfer of charge
TR4	Transfer of a portfolio of charges
TR5	Transfer of portfolio of whole titles
UN1	Application to enter a unilateral notice
UN2	Application to remove a unilateral notice
UN3	Application to be registered as beneficiary of an existing unilateral notice
UN4	Application for the cancellation of a unilateral notice
UT1	Application of upgrading of title
WCT	Application to withdraw a caution

5   TABLE OF LAND REGISTRY PRACTICE GUIDES

Title	*Description and date of issue*
LRPG001	First registrations (1/3/2003)
LRPG002	First registration of title where deeds have been lost or destroyed (1/3/2003)
LRPG003	Cautions against first registration (1/3/2003)